Keep it Simple.   ®   Make it Special.

Easy Classic
Casseroles

Dedication

For every cook who wonders "What's for dinner?"
a little too often!

Appreciation

To all our Gooseberry Patch family & friends who have shared
their favorite casserole recipes with us...thank you!

Gooseberry Patch
An imprint of Globe Pequot
246 Goose Lane • Guilford, CT 06437

www.gooseberrypatch.com

U.S. to Metric Recipe Equivalents

Volume Measurements

1/4 teaspoon	1 mL
1/2 teaspoon	2 mL
1 teaspoon	5 mL
1 tablespoon = 3 teaspoons	15 mL
2 tablespoons = 1 fluid ounce	30 mL
1/4 cup	60 mL
1/3 cup	75 mL
1/2 cup = 4 fluid ounces	125 mL
1 cup = 8 fluid ounces	250 mL
2 cups = 1 pint =16 fluid ounces	500 mL
4 cups = 1 quart	1 L

Weights

1 ounce	30 g
4 ounces	120 g
8 ounces	225 g
16 ounces = 1 pound	450 g

Oven Temperatures

300° F	150° C
325° F	160° C
350° F	180° C
375° F	190° C
400° F	200° C
450° F	230° C

Baking Pan Sizes

Square

8x8x2 inches	2 L = 20x20x5 cm
9x9x2 inches	2.5 L = 23x23x5 cm

Rectangular

13x9x2 inches	3.5 L = 33x23x5 cm

Loaf

9x5x3 inches	2 L = 23x13x7 cm

Round

8x1-1/2 inches	1.2 L = 20x4 cm
9x1-1/2 inches	1.5 L = 23x4 cm

Recipe Abbreviations

t. = teaspoon	ltr. = liter
T. = tablespoon	oz. = ounce
c. = cup	lb. = pound
pt. = pint	doz. = dozen
qt. = quart	pkg. = package
gal. = gallon	env. = envelope

Kitchen Measurements

A pinch = 1/8 tablespoon	1 fluid ounce = 2 tablespoons
3 teaspoons = 1 tablespoon	4 fluid ounces = 1/2 cup
2 tablespoons = 1/8 cup	8 fluid ounces = 1 cup
4 tablespoons = 1/4 cup	16 fluid ounces = 1 pint
8 tablespoons = 1/2 cup	32 fluid ounces = 1 quart
16 tablespoons = 1 cup	16 ounces net weight = 1 pound
2 cups = 1 pint	
4 cups = 1 quart	
4 quarts = 1 gallon	

Table of Contents

Breakfast & Brunch Favorites

From Amish Baked Oatmeal to Sausage & Potato Casserole, this chapter is brimming with recipes to start your day off right. Scalloped Bacon & Eggs, South-of-the-Border Enchiladas, Raisin French Toast Bake and Cheese Blintz Casserole...so many yummy choices, which one will you try first?

Healthy Oatmeal Apple Crisp

Healthy Oatmeal Apple Crisp

Amy Snyder, White Oak, WV

6 c. tart apples, cored and sliced
1/4 c. frozen apple juice concentrate, thawed
1 t. cinnamon, divided
1/4 c. butter, softened
3/4 c. quick-cooking oats, uncooked
1/4 c. whole-wheat flour
1/3 c. brown sugar, packed

In a bowl, combine apples, apple juice concentrate and 1/2 teaspoon cinnamon. Stir until well mixed. Spread in an 8"x8" glass baking pan sprayed with non-stick vegetable spray. In the same bowl, mix remaining cinnamon and other ingredients until crumbly; sprinkle over apples. Bake, uncovered, at 375 degrees for 25 to 35 minutes, until apples are tender and topping is golden. Serve warm. Makes 8 servings.

Ham & Pepper Strata

Howard Cooper, Austin, TX

4 slices French bread, cubed
1 c. cooked ham, diced
1/4 t. red pepper flakes
1/2 green pepper, diced
1 t. dried parsley
4 eggs
1 c. evaporated milk
1 t. mustard
1/2 c. shredded sharp Cheddar cheese

Line the bottom of a greased 8"x8" baking pan with bread; top with ham, red pepper flakes, green pepper and parsley. Set aside. Whisk together eggs, milk, and mustard. Pour evenly over ham; cover tightly with aluminum foil and refrigerate 8 hours to overnight. Bake, covered with foil, at 350 degrees for 55 minutes. Remove foil; sprinkle with cheese and bake for an additional 5 minutes, or until cheese is melted. Serves 4 to 6.

Baked Breakfast Goodness

Kristy Markners, Fort Mill, SC

1/4 c. unsweetened applesauce
1/2 c. sugar or low-calorie powdered sweetener blend for baking
3 T. egg white substitute, beaten
1/2 c. milk or unsweetened almond milk
1-1/2 c. multi-grain hot cereal, uncooked
1 t. baking powder
1/2 t. cinnamon
1/8 t. ground ginger
1 banana, diced
1/4 c. dried wild blueberries

Stir together applesauce, sugar, egg white and milk in a bowl. Add cereal, baking powder and spices; stir until well combined. Fold in fruit. Spoon into an 8"x6" baking pan sprayed with non-stick vegetable spray. Bake, uncovered, at 350 degrees for 30 minutes. Makes 4 servings.

Quick tip

Fresh herbs add savor and color to breakfast dishes. Simply snip herbs directly into eggs or potatoes as they cook. Try chives, dill, thyme and parsley!

Slow-Cooker Breakfast Casserole

Felice Jones, Boise, ID

32-oz. pkg. frozen diced potatoes	1/2 c. shredded Monterey Jack cheese
1 lb. bacon, diced and crisply cooked	1 doz. eggs
1 onion, diced	1 c. milk
1 green pepper, diced	1 t. salt
	1 t. pepper

Layer 1/3 each of potatoes, bacon, onion, green pepper and cheese. Repeat layers 2 more times, ending with a layer of cheese. In a bowl, beat together eggs, milk, salt and pepper. Pour over mixture in slow cooker. Cover and cook on low setting for 8 to 9 hours. Serves 8 to 10.

Slow-Cooker Breakfast Casserole

Bacon & Egg Potato Skins

Dale Duncan, Waterloo, IA

2 baking potatoes	1/4 c. shredded Cheddar cheese
4 eggs, beaten	4 slices bacon, crisply cooked and crumbled
1 to 2 t. butter	
salt and pepper to taste	Optional: sour cream, chopped fresh chives
1/4 c. shredded Monterey Jack cheese	

Bake potatoes at 400 degrees for one hour, until tender. Slice potatoes in half lengthwise; scoop out centers and reserve for another recipe. Place potato skins on a lightly greased baking sheet. Bake at 400 degrees for 6 to 8 minutes, until crisp. Remove from oven. In a skillet over medium heat, scramble eggs in butter just until they begin to set. Add salt and pepper; remove from heat. Spoon equal amounts of eggs, cheese and bacon over each potato skin. Reduce heat to 350 degrees and bake for 10 minutes, until cheese is melted and eggs are completely set. Garnish with sour cream and chives, if desired. Makes 4 servings.

Quick tip

A vintage hand-cranked mini food chopper makes short work of chopping tomatoes, bacon, green onions and chives for topping savory breakfasts.

Bacon & Egg Potato Skins

Brown Sugar-Orange French Toast

Fern Bruner, Palo Alto, CA

4 T. butter, melted	2 T. orange zest
1/4 c. brown sugar, packed	1/8 t. salt
1/2 t. cinnamon	6 to 8 slices French bread
3 eggs, beaten	

Combine butter, brown sugar and cinnamon together in a 13"x9" baking pan and set aside. Blend eggs, orange zest and salt together. Dip bread slices into egg mixture, coating both sides. Arrange dipped bread slices in baking pan. Bake, uncovered, at 400 degrees for 15 to 20 minutes, until golden. Serves 3 to 4.

Brown Sugar-Orange French Toast

Breakfast Apple Pie

Lori Ritchey, Denver, PA

1 egg, beaten	2 apples, cored and cut into wedges
1/4 c. oil	
1 c. milk	1/2 t. cinnamon
1-1/2 c. biscuit baking mix	1/4 t. nutmeg
1/2 c. plus 2 T. sugar, divided	2 T. butter, diced
	Garnish: whipped cream
Optional: 1/2 c. chopped walnuts or pecans	

Beat together egg, oil and milk; add biscuit mix, 1/2 cup sugar and nuts, if using. Beat well. Pour into a greased 9" pie plate. Arrange apple wedges over batter; sprinkle with remaining sugar, cinnamon and nutmeg. Dot with butter. Bake at 375 degrees for 30 minutes, or until apples are tender. Serve warm with whipped cream. Serves 4 to 6.

Tex-Mex Egg Puff

Carol Creed, Battlefield, MO

1 doz. eggs, beaten	1/2 t. salt
2 4-oz. cans chopped green chiles, drained	16-oz. pkg. shredded Monterey Jack cheese
1/2 c. butter, melted and cooled slightly	16-oz. container small-curd cottage cheese
1/2 c. all-purpose flour	
1 t. baking powder	

In a large bowl, whisk together all ingredients. Spoon into a greased 13"x9" baking pan. Bake, uncovered, at 350 degrees for 35 to 40 minutes, until set. Cut into squares. Serves 8 to 10.

Breakfast Apple Pie

Nutty French Toast Bake

Nutty French Toast Bake

Wendy Lee Paffenroth, Pine Island, NY

1 loaf French bread, torn
   into bite-size pieces
1 t. cinnamon
1 c. chopped nuts
1/2 c. raisins
6 eggs, beaten

1 t. vanilla extract
1 c. half-and-half
1 c. milk
1/2 c. maple syrup
1/2 c. brown sugar, packed
1/2 c. butter, melted

Mix bread, cinnamon, nuts and raisins together; spoon into a greased 13"x9" baking pan. Set aside. Beat eggs, vanilla, half-and-half and milk together; stir in maple syrup. Pour over bread; sprinkle with brown sugar. Drizzle with butter; refrigerate for at least one hour. Bake at 350 degrees for 45 minutes to one hour. Serves 6 to 8.

Hearty Breakfast Casserole

Tracie Spencer, Rogers, KY

6 to 8 bread slices
3-oz. pkg. ready-to-use
   bacon crumbles
1 lb. cooked ham, diced,
   or ground pork sausage,
   browned
2 c. shredded Cheddar
   cheese

10 eggs, beaten
1 c. milk
1 t. salt
1 t. pepper

Arrange bread slices in a single layer in a greased 13"x9" baking pan; top with bacon and ham or sausage. Sprinkle with cheese. Whisk together remaining ingredients. Pour egg mixture over top. Cover with aluminum foil and refrigerate overnight. Bake, covered, at 350 degrees for 45 minutes to one hour, until center is set. Serves 12.

Hearty Breakfast Casserole

Quick tip

A weekend morning is the perfect time for an old-fashioned kaffeeklatsch to chat over coffee cake and coffee. Invite a girlfriend or the new neighbor you've been wanting to get to know better. You'll be so glad you did!

Jalapeño Cheese Grits Casserole

Jill Burton, Gooseberry Patch

3 c. quick-cooking grits, uncooked
1/2 c. melted butter, cooled
1/2 c. whipping cream
1 t. salt
16-oz. pkg. shredded Cheddar cheese
4-oz. can diced jalapeños, drained
1 c. mayonnaise
8-oz. pkg. cream cheese, softened
2 green onions, chopped

Cook grits according to package directions. In a bowl, combine grits, butter, cream and salt. In a separate bowl, combine remaining ingredients except onions; mix well. Combine the 2 mixtures; stir together. Pour into a greased 13"x9" baking pan. Bake, uncovered, at 375 degrees for 35 to 40 minutes, until bubbly. Top with onions. Serves 8.

Upside-Down Eggs & Potatoes

Jessica Dekoekkoek, Richmond, VA

2 to 3 T. olive oil
1 to 2 potatoes, shredded
1-1/2 t. garlic powder
1-1/2 t. onion powder
1/2 t. paprika
1-1/2 c. shredded Mexican-blend cheese
6 eggs
salt and pepper to taste
Garnish: sour cream, salsa

Heat oil in a deep 12" oven-proof skillet over medium heat. Pat potatoes dry; add seasonings and toss to mix. Add potatoes to skillet. When about half cooked, use the back of a wooden spoon to smooth out potatoes over the bottom and up the sides of the skillet, to form a crust with no holes. Add cheese in an even layer. Beat eggs very well; add salt and pepper to taste. Gently pour in eggs over cheese. Bake, uncovered, at 375 degrees for 25 to 35 minutes, until a knife tip comes out clean. Carefully unmold onto a serving plate. Let stand for 10 minutes before cutting into wedges. Serve with sour cream and salsa. Makes 6 servings.

Quick tip

Looking for a quick, no-mess way to cook bacon? Arrange bacon slices on a broiler pan and place the pan 3 to 4 inches from the preheated broiler. Broil for one to 2 minutes on each side, depending on how crispy you like your bacon.

Upside-Down Eggs & Potatoes

Cheesy Hashbrown Casserole

Cheesy Hashbrown Casserole

Crystal MacLean, Camrose, Alberta

4 c. frozen diced potatoes

1 c. sour cream

10-3/4 oz. can cream of mushroom soup

2 c. shredded Cheddar cheese

1/8 t. pepper

Optional: 1 T. onion, finely chopped

Garnish: grated Parmesan cheese

In a large bowl, mix together all ingredients except garnish. Spoon into a greased 8"x8" glass baking pan. Sprinkle lightly with Parmesan cheese. Bake, uncovered, at 350 degrees for one hour, or until center is hot and sides are bubbly. May also be made a day ahead, covered and refrigerated, then baked in the morning. Serves 6.

Blueberry & Cream Cheese Strata

Kathy Grashoff, Fort Wayne, IN

16-oz. loaf white bread, crusts removed, cubed and divided

2 c. frozen blueberries, divided

3-oz. pkg. cream cheese, cut into 1/4-inch cubes

4 eggs

2 c. milk

1/3 c. sugar

1 t. vanilla extract

1/4 t. salt

1/4 t. nutmeg

Place half of the bread in a greased 8"x8" baking pan; top with half of the blueberries. Top with cream cheese, remaining bread and remaining blueberries; set aside. Beat eggs, milk, sugar, vanilla, salt and nutmeg with an electric mixer on medium speed until blended. Pour over bread mixture and refrigerate for 20 minutes to overnight. Bake, uncovered, at 325 degrees for one hour. Serves 4 to 6.

Blueberry & Cream Cheese Strata

French Toast Soufflé

Marybeth Biggins, Brockton, MA

10 c. bread, cubed

8-oz. pkg. cream cheese, softened

8 eggs

1-1/2 c. milk

2/3 c. half-and-half

1/2 c. maple syrup

1/2 t. vanilla extract

3/4 t. cinnamon

2 T. powdered sugar

Place bread in a greased 13"x9" baking pan; set aside. Beat cream cheese until smooth; add eggs. Mix well; stir in milk, half-and-half, maple syrup, vanilla and cinnamon. Blend until smooth; pour over bread. Bake at 375 degrees for 50 minutes; sprinkle with powdered sugar. Serves 6 to 8.

Sausage & Potato Casserole

Megan Heep, Chicago, IL

1/4 c. oil
1/2 c. all-purpose flour
2 t. salt
1/4 t. pepper
4 c. milk

8 to 10 potatoes, boiled
  and sliced
1 lb. ground sausage,
  browned
1 c. shredded American
  cheese

Combine oil, flour, salt and pepper in a large skillet. Cook and stir over medium heat until hot. Whisk in milk, stirring constantly, until thickened; remove from heat. Layer half of potatoes, flour mixture and sausage into an ungreased 13"x9" baking pan; repeat layers. Sprinkle cheese on top. Bake, uncovered, at 350 degrees for 30 minutes or until cheese begins to brown slightly. Makes 8 to 10 servings.

Quick tip

Salt & pepper is a must with scrambled eggs, crispy hashbrowns and other tasty breakfast foods. Look for whimsical shakers for a sweet rise & shine greeting at the breakfast table.

Sausage & Potato Casserole

Crescent Breakfast Casserole

Tammy Walker, Kansas City, MO

8-oz. tube refrigerated
  crescent rolls
6 to 8 eggs, beaten
1/4 c. milk
3/4 c. finely shredded
  Cheddar cheese
1/2 c. bacon or ground
  pork sausage, cooked and
  crumbled
salt and pepper to taste

Line the bottom and sides of a lightly greased 13"x9" baking pan with unrolled crescents, pinching seams together to seal. In a bowl, mix together remaining ingredients. Pour over dough in baking pan. Bake at 350 degrees for about 20 minutes, until golden and center is set. Serves 8.

Eggnog French Toast Strata

Sandy Bogan, Waldorf, MD

1 loaf French bread, sliced
3-oz. pkg. cream cheese,
  softened
2-1/2 c. eggnog
6 T. butter, melted
8 eggs, beaten
1/4 t. nutmeg

Arrange enough bread slices to cover the bottom of a greased 13"x9" baking pan. Spread cream cheese over bread; arrange remaining bread over top. Whisk together eggnog, butter and eggs until blended. Pour evenly over bread. With back of spoon, gently press bread into dish. Sprinkle with nutmeg. Cover and refrigerate for 8 hours to overnight. Uncover; bake at 325 degrees for 30 to 35 minutes, until center is set and edges are golden. Let stand for 10 minutes; cut into squares. Serve with Cranberry Syrup. Makes 6 to 8 servings.

Cranberry Syrup:

1 c. frozen raspberry juice
  concentrate, thawed
1/3 c. sugar
1 c. whole-berry cranberry
  sauce

Combine in a saucepan over low heat. Cook and whisk until bubbly.

Blueberry Oatmeal Crisp

Blueberry Oatmeal Crisp

Amy Bastian, Mifflinburg, PA

4 c. blueberries
1 c. all-purpose flour,
  divided
3/4 c. brown sugar, packed
3/4 c. long-cooking oats,
  uncooked
1/2 t. cinnamon
1/4 t. nutmeg
5 to 6 T. butter

Combine blueberries with 1/4 cup flour in a greased 11"x7" baking pan; mix thoroughly. In a bowl, combine remaining flour and other ingredients except butter. Cut in butter until coarse crumbs form; sprinkle over blueberries. Bake at 350 degrees for 25 minutes, or until top is golden and blueberries are bubbly. Makes 6 to 8 servings.

Artichoke Frittata

Karen Lee Puchnick, Butler, PA

2 6-oz. jars marinated
 artichokes, drained and
 2 T. marinade reserved
4 eggs, beaten
1 c. ricotta cheese
1 onion, chopped
1/8 t. dried rosemary
1/8 t. dried thyme
1/8 t. dried basil
1/8 t. dried marjoram

Finely chop artichokes; place in a bowl. Add reserved marinade and remaining ingredients; mix well. Spread mixture into a greased 8"x8" baking pan. Bake at 350 degrees for 30 minutes, or until set and golden. Cut into one-inch squares; serve warm. Serves 6 to 8.

Artichoke Frittata

Peachy Baked Oatmeal

Hannah Hilgendorf, Nashotah, WI

2 eggs, beaten
1/2 c. brown sugar, packed
1-1/2 t. baking powder
1/4 t. salt
1-1/2 t. cinnamon
1/2 t. nutmeg
1-1/2 t. vanilla extract
3/4 c. milk
3 c. long-cooking oats,
 uncooked
1/3 c. oil
16-oz. can sliced peaches,
 partially drained
Garnish: warm milk

In a bowl, combine eggs, brown sugar, baking powder, salt, spices and vanilla; beat well. Add remaining ingredients except garnish; mix thoroughly. Spoon into a greased 8"x8" baking pan. Bake at 375 degrees for 20 to 25 minutes, until center is set. Serve in bowls, topped with warm milk. Serves 6.

Make-Ahead French Toast

Carla Turner, Salem, OR

5 T. margarine
2 baking apples, peeled,
 cored and sliced
1 c. brown sugar, packed
2 T. dark corn syrup
1 t. cinnamon
8 1-inch thick slices
 French bread
3 eggs, beaten
1 c. milk
1 t. vanilla extract

Melt margarine in a heavy skillet over medium heat. Reduce heat to medium-low; add apples and cook, stirring occasionally, until tender. Stir in brown sugar, corn syrup and cinnamon. Cook and stir until brown sugar dissolves. Pour apple mixture into two lightly greased 9" pie plates or one, 13"x9" baking pan. Arrange bread slices in one layer on top of apple mixture; set aside. In a medium bowl, whisk together remaining ingredients; pour over bread slices. Cover with plastic wrap and refrigerate overnight. Remove plastic wrap and bake at 375 degrees for 30 to 35 minutes, or until firm and golden. Cool 5 minutes in pan, then invert onto a serving platter. Serves 12 to 15.

Peachy Baked Oatmeal

Pecan French Toast

Pecan French Toast

Darcie Stearns, Rock Island, IL

1 loaf French bread, sliced
6 eggs
1-1/2 c. milk
1-1/2 c. half-and-half
1 t. vanilla extract
1/8 t. nutmeg
1 t. cinnamon

Arrange bread in a lightly greased 13"x9" baking pan; set aside. Beat together remaining ingredients; pour over bread. Cover; refrigerate overnight. Spread Topping over mixture; bake at 350 degrees for 45 to 55 minutes. Let stand 5 minutes before serving. Serves 6 to 8.

Topping:

1/2 c. butter, softened
2 T. maple syrup
1 c. brown sugar, packed
1 c. chopped pecans

Mix all ingredients together.

Crab, Corn & Pepper Frittata

Crab, Corn & Pepper Frittata

Stacie Avner, Delaware, OH

6 eggs, beaten
1/4 c. milk
1/3 c. mayonnaise
1 c. imitation crabmeat
2 T. green onion, chopped
2 T. red pepper, chopped
1/3 c. corn
salt and pepper to taste
1 c. shredded Monterey Jack cheese

Whisk together all ingredients except cheese. Pour into a greased 10" pie plate. Bake at 350 degrees for 15 to 20 minutes. Sprinkle with cheese and bake for an additional 5 minutes, or until cheese is melted. Serves 4 to 6.

Southern-Style Spoonbread

Sharon Tillman, Hampton, VA

3 c. milk
1-1/2 c. yellow cornmeal
1/2 c. butter, diced and softened
2 t. baking powder
5 eggs, separated
1 c. cooked country ham, diced

Bring milk to a slow boil in a large saucepan; gradually add cornmeal, stirring constantly. Reduce to low heat and cook, stirring constantly, for 10 minutes, until thickened. Remove from heat; add butter and baking powder and stir until butter is melted. Let cool and set aside. Beat egg yolks until light with a fork in a small bowl; stir into cooled cornmeal mixture. Add ham and mix until blended; set aside. Beat egg whites with an electric mixer on medium speed until stiff peaks form; fold into cornmeal mixture until well combined. Pour into a greased 2-quart casserole dish; bake at 350 degrees until a toothpick inserted in the center comes out clean, about 40 minutes. Makes 6 to 8 servings.

Sausage & Pecan Casserole

Elizabeth Smithson, Cunningham, KY

8-oz. pkg. pork breakfast sausage links
16-oz. loaf cinnamon bread, cubed
6 eggs, beaten
1-1/2 c. half-and-half
1-1/2 c. milk
1 t. vanilla extract
1 c. chopped pecans
1/2 t. cinnamon
1/2 t. nutmeg

Brown sausages in a skillet over medium heat; drain and thinly slice. Place bread cubes in a 13"x9" baking pan sprayed with non-stick vegetable spray. Top with sausages and set aside. In a bowl, beat together remaining ingredients. Pour egg mixture over sausage; press down gently. Cover and refrigerate overnight. In the morning, make Topping; sprinkle over top. Bake, uncovered, at 350 degrees for 35 minutes, or until bubbly and eggs are set. Serves 10.

Topping:

1 c. brown sugar, packed
1 c. chopped pecans
1/2 c. butter, softened
2 T. maple syrup

Stir together all ingredients with a fork until crumbly.

Quick tip

Shh...here's the secret to flaky homemade biscuits! Don't overmix or overwork the dough...just stir to mix and roll or pat out gently.

Raisin French Toast Bake

Jill Ball, Highland, UT

5 c. cinnamon raisin bread, cubed
4 eggs, beaten
1-1/2 c. milk
1/4 c. sugar
1 t. vanilla extract
3 T. butter, cubed and softened
2 t. cinnamon

Place bread cubes in a lightly buttered 8"x8" baking pan. In a bowl, beat together eggs, milk, sugar and vanilla until mixed. Pour mixture over bread cubes. Dot with butter. Let stand about 10 minutes, until bread has absorbed liquid. Sprinkle with cinnamon. Bake at 350 degrees until golden on top, 45 to 50 minutes. Serve warm. Makes 6 servings.

Cheese Blintz Casserole

Tori Willis, Champaign, IL

1-1/4 c. all-purpose flour
1 t. baking powder
3 T. sugar
1/2 c. plus 2 T. butter, softened and divided
3/4 c. milk
3 eggs, divided
16-oz. container cottage cheese
1 T. sour cream
1/2 t. salt

Combine flour, baking powder, sugar and 1/2 cup butter in a medium bowl. Mix well; stir in milk and 2 eggs. Set aside. Stir together cottage cheese, sour cream, salt, remaining butter and egg in a separate bowl; set aside. Spoon half the flour mixture into a lightly greased 9"x9" baking pan; top with cottage cheese mixture, then with remaining flour mixture. Bake at 350 degrees for 50 minutes, or until puffy and golden. Let cool slightly; cut into squares. Serves 6.

Sausage & Pecan Casserole

Bacon-Mushroom Frittata

Bacon-Mushroom Frittata

April Jacobs, Loveland, CO

8 slices bacon, crisply
  cooked and crumbled
2 c. sliced mushrooms
1 c. onion, chopped
6 eggs, beaten

3/4 c. sour cream
1 t. fresh oregano, chopped
salt and pepper to taste
1/3 c. shredded Cheddar
  cheese

In a cast-iron skillet over medium heat, cook bacon until crisp. Drain bacon on paper towels. Add mushrooms and onion to drippings in skillet. Cook for about 5 minutes, until mushrooms are golden and onion is translucent; drain and remove from heat. In a separate bowl, whisk together eggs, sour cream, seasonings and mushroom mixture. Pour egg mixture into same skillet or a lightly greased 9" pie plate. Sprinkle evenly with crumbled bacon. Bake at 425 degrees for 15 minutes. Reduce heat to 300 degrees; bake an additional 10 minutes, or until eggs are completely set. Remove from oven. Sprinkle with cheese; let stand 5 minutes. Slice into wedges; serve warm. Makes 4 to 6 servings.

Scalloped Bacon & Eggs

Scalloped Bacon & Eggs

Rita Morgan, Pueblo, CO

1/4 c. onion, chopped
2 T. butter
2 T. all-purpose flour
1-1/2 c. milk
1 c. shredded Cheddar
  cheese
1/2 t. dry mustard
6 eggs, hard-boiled, peeled
  and sliced

1/2 t. salt
1/4 t. pepper
1-1/2 c. potato chips,
  crushed
10 slices bacon, crisply
  cooked and crumbled

In a skillet over medium heat, sauté onion in butter until translucent; stir in flour. Gradually add milk and cook, stirring constantly, until thickened. Add cheese and mustard, stirring until cheese melts. Place half the egg slices in a greased 8"x8" baking pan. Sprinkle with salt and pepper. Cover with half each of the cheese sauce, potato chips and bacon. Repeat layers. Bake, uncovered, at 350 degrees for 15 to 20 minutes. Serves 4 to 6.

Quick tip

A wire basket full of brown eggs makes a terrific farm-style breakfast centerpiece. For a seasonal touch, fill the basket with mini white eggplants or egg-shaped gourds.

Savory Zucchini Frittata

Jacqueline Young-De Roover, San Francisco, CA

2 T. olive oil

3 shallots, finely minced

4 cloves garlic, finely minced

6 zucchini, sliced 1/4-inch thick on the diagonal

1 doz. eggs, lightly beaten

salt and white pepper to taste

1 c. fresh Italian flat-leaf parsley, snipped

1 c. finely shredded Parmesan cheese

Add oil to a large skillet over medium heat; swirl to coat bottom and sides of pan. Add shallots and garlic; cook and stir for about one minute. Add zucchini; cook, stirring often, for 5 to 7 minutes, until crisp-tender.

Savory Zucchini Frittata

Remove pan from heat; add remaining ingredients and mix lightly. Spray a 9" round glass baking pan with butter-flavored non-stick vegetable spray. Spoon mixture into pan. Bake, uncovered, at 325 degrees until set, about 30 minutes. Serve warm or cooled. Makes 6 servings.

Egg & Mushroom Bake

Debbie Foster, Eastover, SC

1 doz. eggs, beaten and scrambled

8-oz. pkg. sliced mushrooms

10-3/4 oz. can cream of mushroom soup

2/3 c. milk

8-oz. jar bacon bits

1-1/2 c. shredded Cheddar cheese

Spread eggs in the bottom of a greased 1-1/2 quart casserole dish; top with mushrooms. Set aside. Combine soup and milk in a microwave-safe bowl; heat in a microwave oven on high for 3 minutes, stirring after each minute. Pour over mushrooms; sprinkle with bacon bits and Cheddar cheese. Bake at 350 degrees for 30 minutes. Serves 4.

Morning Delight

Jane White, Kountze, TX

2 8-oz. tubes refrigerated crescent rolls, divided

2 8-oz. pkgs. cream cheese, softened

1 egg

1 T. almond extract

1 c. sugar

Garnish: sugar, cinnamon to taste

Press one tube of crescent rolls into the bottom of a greased 13"x9" baking pan; seal seams. Set aside. Mix cream cheese, egg, extract and sugar in a bowl; spread over rolls in pan. Top with remaining crescent rolls; sprinkle to taste with sugar and cinnamon. Bake at 350 degrees for 20 to 25 minutes, or until golden. Serves 6 to 8.

Egg & Mushroom Bake

Baked Eggs in Tomatoes

Baked Eggs in Tomatoes

Jill Burton, Gooseberry Patch

6 tomatoes, tops cut off
  and reserved

salt and pepper to taste

1/2 c. corn, thawed if
  frozen

1/2 c. red pepper, diced

1/2 c. mushrooms, diced

2 T. cream cheese,
  softened and divided

6 eggs

2 t. fresh chives, minced

1/4 c. grated Parmesan
  cheese

With a spoon, carefully scoop out each tomato, creating shells. Sprinkle salt and pepper inside tomatoes. Divide corn, red pepper and mushrooms among tomatoes; top each with one teaspoon cream cheese. In a bowl, whisk together eggs, chives and additional salt and pepper. Divide egg mixture among tomatoes; top with Parmesan cheese. Place tomatoes in a lightly greased 9"x9" baking pan; replace tops on tomatoes. Bake, uncovered, at 350 degrees until egg mixture is set, about 45 to 50 minutes. Serve warm. Makes 6 servings.

Gold Rush Brunch

Kim McCorry, Rochester Hills, MI

15-1/2 oz. pkg. frozen
  shredded hashbrowns
  with onions and peppers

1/4 c. butter

1/4 c. all-purpose flour

1/2 t. salt

1/8 t. pepper

2 c. milk

1 c. sour cream

2 T. fresh parsley, minced

8 slices Canadian bacon

8 eggs

Prepare hashbrowns according to package directions; set aside. Melt butter in a saucepan; blend in flour, salt and pepper. Stir in milk; cook until bubbly. Remove from heat; stir in sour cream, parsley and hashbrowns. Spoon into a greased 13"x9" baking pan; arrange bacon in the center. Bake at 350 degrees for 20 minutes; remove from oven. Make 8 depressions in mixture; place one egg in each. Bake for an additional 10 to 12 minutes. Serves 8.

Amish Baked Oatmeal

Emily Nussbaum, Massillon, OH

1/4 c. butter, softened

1 egg, beaten

1/2 c. sugar

1 t. baking powder

1/2 t. salt

1/2 c. milk

1 t. vanilla extract

2 T. oil

1-3/4 c. quick-cooking oats,
  uncooked

Mix the first 8 ingredients together until smooth; pour into a greased 13"x9" baking pan. Stir in oats; bake at 350 degrees for 30 to 35 minutes. Serves 6 to 8.

Finnish Pancakes

Corinne Ficek, Normal, IL

3 T. butter, melted

4 eggs

2 c. milk

1 c. all-purpose flour

1/8 t. salt

1 T. sugar

1 t. vanilla extract

Melt butter in a 13"x9" baking pan in the oven at 400 degrees; set aside. Place eggs in a blender; blend well. Add milk, flour, salt, sugar and vanilla; blend thoroughly. Pour into pan; bake at 400 degrees for 35 minutes. Serves 4.

3-Cheese Western Omelet

Jane Skillin, Montclair, NJ

3/4 c. mild salsa

1 c. artichoke hearts,
  chopped

1/4 c. grated Parmesan
  cheese

1 c. shredded Monterey
  Jack cheese

1 c. shredded Cheddar
  cheese

6 eggs

1 c. sour cream

Spread salsa in the bottom of a greased 10" pie plate. Sprinkle artichokes over salsa; top with cheeses. Set aside. Blend eggs and sour cream together; spread over cheeses. Bake at 350 degrees for 30 minutes, or until set. Cut into wedges to serve. Makes 6 servings.

Breakfast & Brunch Favorites

Zesty Sausage Burritos

Joshua Logan, Corpus Christi, TX

2 lbs. ground sausage

1 doz. eggs, beaten

4-oz. can chopped green chiles

8-oz. pkg. shredded Cheddar cheese

8 10-inch flour tortillas

1 T. all-purpose flour

1 c. milk

Brown sausage in a skillet over medium heat. Drain; reserve 2 tablespoons drippings in skillet and set sausage aside. Add eggs and chiles to skillet; cook and stir until eggs are done. Set aside. Divide sausage, cheese and egg equally among tortillas. Roll up tortillas and place seam-side down in a lightly greased 13"x9" baking pan; set aside. Heat reserved drippings in skillet. Sprinkle with flour; stir. Add milk, stirring constantly, until mixture begins to thicken; pour over tortillas. Bake at 350 degrees for 10 to 15 minutes, until hot and bubbly. Serves 6.

Goldenrod Bake

Jackie Smulski, Lyons, IL

2 T. butter

1/2 t. paprika

salt and pepper to taste

2 T. all-purpose flour

1 c. milk

3/4 c. shredded Cheddar cheese

4 to 6 eggs, hard-boiled, peeled and chopped

1/4 c. dry bread crumbs

1 t. fresh chives, snipped

bread triangles or English muffin halves, toasted

Melt butter in a saucepan; whisk in paprika, salt and pepper. Remove from heat; whisk in flour. Return to low heat; stir in milk, whisking continually until sauce thickens. Remove from heat; stir in cheese until melted. Add eggs; mix well. Pour mixture into a lightly greased 9"x9" baking pan sprayed with butter-flavored non-stick vegetable spray. Top with bread crumbs and chives. Bake at 350 degrees for 15 to 20 minutes, until bubbly. Spoon over toasted bread or English muffins. Serves 4 to 6.

Best Brunch Casserole

Lita Hardy, Santa Cruz, CA

4 c. croutons

2 c. shredded Cheddar cheese

8 eggs, beaten

4 c. milk

1 t. salt

1 t. pepper

2 t. mustard

1 T. dried, minced onion

6 slices bacon, crisply cooked and crumbled

Spread croutons in a greased 13"x9" baking pan; sprinkle with cheese and set aside. In a bowl, whisk together remaining ingredients except bacon; pour over cheese. Sprinkle bacon on top. Bake, uncovered, at 325 degrees for 55 to 60 minutes, until set. Serves 8.

Quick tip

Start a collection of retro jelly-jar juice glasses...their fun designs and bright colors will make everyone smile at breakfast time.

Zesty Sausage Burritos

Mom's Red Flannel Hash

Mom's Red Flannel Hash

Phyllis Peters, Three Rivers, MI

12-oz. can corned beef,
  coarsely chopped
2 c. beets, peeled, cooked
  and chopped
2 c. potatoes, peeled,
  cooked and chopped
1/2 c. butter, melted

Toss all ingredients together. Pour into a greased 2-quart casserole dish. Bake, uncovered, at 350 degrees for 40 minutes. Makes 4 to 6 servings.

Garden Bounty Egg Bake

Lisa Sanders, Shoals, IN

1 doz. eggs
1/2 c. milk
1 T. dried parsley
1 t. dried thyme
1 t. garlic powder
salt and pepper to taste
1 T. olive oil
8-oz. pkg. sliced
  mushrooms
1/2 c. onion, diced
1/2 c. green pepper, diced
1/2 c. carrot, peeled and
  shredded
1/2 c. broccoli, chopped
1/2 c. tomato, chopped
1 c. shredded mild
  Cheddar cheese
Optional: hot pepper sauce

In a bowl, whisk together eggs and milk; stir in seasonings and set aside. Heat oil in a large ovenproof skillet over medium-high heat. Add all vegetables except tomato; sauté until crisp-tender. Add tomato to skillet. Pour egg mixture over vegetable mixture; remove skillet to the oven. Bake at 350 degrees for about 15 to 20 minutes, until a knife tip inserted in the center tests clean. Sprinkle with cheese; return to oven until cheese melts. Serve with hot pepper sauce, if desired. Makes 6 servings.

Savory Egg Bake

Janice Barr, Lincoln, NE

3 eggs, beaten
1/4 c. sour cream
1/4 t. salt
1 tomato, chopped
1 green onion, sliced
1/4 c. shredded Cheddar
  cheese

In a small bowl, beat eggs, sour cream and salt together.

Stir in tomato, onion and cheese. Pour into a greased 2-cup casserole dish or ramekin. Bake, uncovered, at 350 degrees for 25 to 30 minutes, until a knife tip inserted in center tests clean. Serves 2.

French Toast Casserole

Lori Hurley, Fishers, IN

1 c. brown sugar, packed
1/2 c. butter
2 c. corn syrup
1 loaf French bread, sliced
5 eggs, beaten
1-1/2 c. milk
1 t. vanilla extract
Garnish: powdered sugar,
  maple syrup

Melt together brown sugar, butter and corn syrup in a saucepan over low heat; pour into a greased 13"x9" baking pan. Arrange bread slices over mixture and set aside. Whisk together eggs, milk and vanilla; pour over bread, coating all slices. Cover and refrigerate overnight. Uncover and bake at 350 degrees for 30minutes, or until lightly golden. Sprinkle with powdered sugar; serve with warm syrup. Makes 6 to 8 servings.

Clean-Out-the-Fridge Frittata

Cindy Kemp, Lake Jackson, TX

6 eggs
1/2 c. water
1/2 c. cooked meats, cut
  into bite-size pieces
1/2 c. cooked vegetables,
  cut into bite-size pieces
1/4 c. salsa
Optional: 1/4 c. sliced
  mushrooms
salt and pepper to taste
1 c. shredded Cheddar
  or mozzarella cheese,
  divided

In a large bowl, whisk eggs until well beaten. Add water and whisk well. Add remaining ingredients except cheese. Mix well and stir in 1/2 cup cheese. Pour mixture into a cast-iron skillet or a one-quart casserole dish that has been sprayed with non-stick vegetable spray. Top with remaining cheese. Bake, uncovered, at 400 degrees for about 30 to 40 minutes, until center is set. Makes 6 to 8 servings.

Cinnamon-Apple Pancake

Cinnamon-Apple Pancake

Vickie

4 apples, peeled, cored and sliced
1/2 c. butter, softened and divided
1/2 c. brown sugar, packed
1 t. cinnamon
1/8 t. nutmeg
6 eggs
1 c. all-purpose flour
1 c. milk
3 T. sugar
Optional: warm maple syrup

Combine apples, 1/4 cup butter, brown sugar, cinnamon and nutmeg in a microwave-safe bowl; heat on high setting about 2 to 4 minutes, until tender. Spoon into a lightly greased 13"x9" baking pan and set aside. Combine eggs, flour, milk, sugar and remaining butter; blend until smooth and spread over apple mixture. Bake at 425 degrees for 25 minutes. Top with syrup if desired. Serves 6 to 8.

Toffee Apple French Toast

Patricia Wissler, Harrisburg, PA

8 c. French bread, sliced into 1-inch cubes and divided
2 Granny Smith apples, cored, peeled and chopped
8-oz. pkg. cream cheese, softened
3/4 c. brown sugar, packed
1/4 c. sugar
1-3/4 c. milk, divided
2 t. vanilla extract, divided
1/2 c. toffee or almond brickle baking bits
5 eggs, beaten

Place half the bread cubes in a greased 13"x9" baking pan; top with apples and set aside. In a medium bowl, beat cream cheese, sugars, 1/4 cup milk and one teaspoon vanilla until smooth. Stir in baking bits and spread over apples. Top with remaining bread cubes. In a separate bowl, beat eggs with remaining milk and vanilla; pour over bread. Cover and refrigerate for 8 hours to overnight. Remove from refrigerator 30 minutes before baking. Uncover and bake at 350 degrees for 35 to 45 minutes, until a knife inserted near the center comes out clean. Makes 8 servings.

Applesauce Baked Oatmeal

Laura Wirsig, Holden, MO

1-1/2 c. quick-cooking oats, uncooked
1/4 c. sugar
1 t. baking powder
3/4 t. salt
1/2 c. milk
1/4 c. butter, softened
1 egg, beaten
1/4 c. applesauce
1 t. vanilla extract
Optional: warm milk, brown sugar, sliced fruit

Combine oats, sugar, baking powder and salt; mix well. Add remaining ingredients except optional ones; mix to a smooth, thin consistency. Spread evenly in a greased 13"x9" baking pan. Bake, uncovered, at 350 degrees for 25 to 30 minutes, until edges turn golden. Serve immediately by spooning into individual bowls. Add additional warmed milk, if needed for desired consistency. Top with brown sugar or sliced fruit, as desired. Makes 6 to 8 servings.

South-of-the-Border Enchiladas

Mexican Brunch Casserole

Olive Herzberg, Lomita, CA

2 4-oz. cans whole green chiles, drained
2 to 3 tomatoes, chopped
2 c. shredded Colby Jack cheese
1 c. biscuit baking mix
3 eggs
1 c. milk
1/2 t. salt

In a lightly greased 8"x8" baking pan, layer chiles, tomatoes and cheese. Beat together remaining ingredients and spoon over cheese. Bake, uncovered, at 375 degrees for 30 to 35 minutes, until set. Serves 3 to 4.

Baked Blueberry Oatmeal

Sharon Newell, Hancock, MI

4 c. old-fashioned oats, uncooked
1 c. sugar
2 t. baking powder
2 c. milk
3/4 c. butter, melted and slightly cooled
4 eggs, beaten
3/4 c. applesauce
1 c. blueberries, thawed if frozen
Optional: brown sugar

In a large bowl, mix together all ingredients except blueberries and brown sugar. Spoon into a lightly greased 13"x9" baking pan. Add blueberries; push down into mixture. If desired, sprinkle brown sugar on top. Bake, uncovered, at 350 degrees for 40 minutes, or until golden on top. Makes 8 servings.

South-of-the-Border Enchiladas

Connie Hilty, Pearland, TX

1 T. oil
16-oz. pkg. frozen shredded hashbrowns
1 c. cooked ham, diced
4-1/2 oz. can diced green chiles
1-1/2 c. shredded Cheddar cheese, divided
28-oz. can green chile enchilada sauce, divided
8 10-inch flour tortillas

Heat oil in a skillet over medium-high heat. Add hashbrowns and ham; cook until golden. Stir in chiles and 1/2 cup cheese until cheese is melted. Spoon enough enchilada sauce into an ungreased 13"x9" baking pan to coat the bottom. Dip each tortilla in remaining sauce and fill with hashbrown mixture. Roll each tortilla as tightly as possible and place in baking pan seam-side down. Top with remaining sauce and cheese; cover with aluminum foil. Bake at 375 degrees for about 20 minutes. Remove foil and bake an additional 10 minutes, or until lightly golden. Serve immediately. Serves 8.

Quick tip

For best results when baking, preheat the oven first. Turn on the oven and set it to the correct temperature at least 15 minutes ahead of time.

Ham & Broccoli Breakfast Bake

Ham & Broccoli Breakfast Bake

Jo Ann

1 doz. eggs
2 c. milk
1/2 t. garlic powder
1/2 t. dried oregano
1/8 t. pepper
1 c. cooked ham, finely
   diced

2 c. broccoli, cooked and
   chopped
1/4 c. onion, finely diced
2 c. shredded Cheddar
   cheese

In a large bowl, with an electric mixer on low speed, beat eggs and milk well. Stir in seasonings with a spoon; set aside. Sprinkle remaining ingredients evenly into a 13"x9" baking pan sprayed with non-stick vegetable spray. Slowly pour egg mixture into pan. Bake, uncovered, at 350 degrees for 45 to 50 minutes, until golden and a knife tip inserted in center tests clean. Allow to cool slightly before cutting into squares. Makes 8 servings.

Lazy Man's Pancakes

Mel Chencharick, Julian, PA

3 T. butter
6 eggs
1-1/2 c. milk
1-1/2 c. all-purpose flour

3/4 t. salt
Optional: chopped
   walnuts, maple syrup

Melt butter in a 13"x9" baking pan placed in a 425-degree oven. Meanwhile, in a bowl, combine eggs, milk, flour and salt; beat well. Slowly pour mixture into buttered pan. Bake at 425 degrees for 20 to 25 minutes, until top is golden. Cut into squares; serve topped with nuts and syrup, if desired. Serves 5 to 6.

Denver Oven Omelet

Charlene McCain, Bakersfield, CA

8 eggs, beaten
1/2 c. half-and-half
1 c. shredded Cheddar
   cheese
1 c. cooked ham, chopped

1/4 c. green pepper,
   chopped
1/4 c. onion, finely
   chopped
salt and pepper to taste

Lazy Man's Pancakes

In a large bowl, whisk eggs and half-and-half until light and fluffy. Stir in remaining ingredients. Pour into a greased 9"x9" baking pan. Bake, uncovered, at 400 degrees for 25 minutes, or until set and golden. Serves 4.

Easy Breakfast Squares

Vicki Hirsch, Platteville, WI

24-oz. pkg. frozen
   shredded hashbrowns
1-1/2 c. shredded
   mozzarella cheese
1-1/2 c. shredded Cheddar
   cheese

1 onion, diced
2 c. cooked ham, diced
salt and pepper to taste
3 eggs
1 c. milk

In a lightly greased 13"x9" baking pan, layer hashbrowns, cheeses, onion and ham; season with salt and pepper. Set aside. In a bowl, beat together eggs and milk; pour over ham. Cover; refrigerate 8 hours to overnight. Uncover; bake at 350 degrees for 45 minutes. Cut into squares to serve. Serves 6 to 8.

Chapter 2

Quick-Fix Recipes

Need to whip up a delicious meal in a jiffy? We've got a bushel full of quick-to-fix recipes just for you. Some feature just a few simple ingredients, others feature shorter cooking times. One thing's for sure...every recipe is scrumptious!

Crunchy Chicken Casserole

Crunchy Chicken Casserole

Kendra Keierleber, Lubbock, TX

6-oz. pkg. wild rice, uncooked

14-1/2 oz. can French-style green beans, drained

10-3/4 oz. can cream of chicken soup

1/2 c. mayonnaise

4 boneless, skinless chicken breasts, cooked

8-oz. can sliced water chestnuts, drained

1 oz. slivered almonds

2 c. shredded mild Cheddar cheese

Cook rice 5 minutes less than directed on package; mix with remaining ingredients, except cheese. Pour into a greased 13"x9" baking pan. Top with cheese. Bake at 350 degrees for 30 minutes. Makes 4 servings.

Quick Tuna Casserole

Debbi Corlew, Colona, IL

2 6-oz. cans tuna, drained

10-3/4 oz. can cream of mushroom soup

3/4 c. milk

1 T. Worcestershire sauce

hot pepper sauce to taste

1 sleeve round buttery crackers, crushed

In a bowl, mix together all ingredients except crackers; set aside. In a greased 9"x9" baking pan, layer one-third of crackers and top with half of tuna mixture. Repeat layers; top with remaining crackers and more hot sauce, if desired. Bake, uncovered, at 350 degrees for 30 minutes, or until hot and bubbly. Serves 4.

Quick Tuna Casserole

Quick tip

For dark, rich-looking gravy, add a spoonful or two of brewed coffee. It will add color to pale gravy but won't affect the flavor.

Fast & Fresh Asparagus Casserole

Kelly Alderson, Erie, PA

1 lb. carrots, peeled, sliced and cooked

15-oz. can asparagus spears, drained

15-1/4 oz. can peas, drained

8-oz. can sliced water chestnuts, drained

3 eggs, hard-boiled, peeled and sliced

1/3 c. butter

10-3/4 oz. can cream of mushroom soup

1 c. shredded Cheddar cheese, divided

1 c. cracker crumbs

1/2 t. pepper

Layer carrots, asparagus and peas in a lightly greased 13"x9" baking pan. Place water chestnuts and sliced eggs over vegetables. Dot with butter. Mix soup and 3/4 cup cheese; spread over vegetable layers. Bake at 350 degrees for 30 minutes, or until bubbly. Sprinkle with crumbs, pepper and remaining cheese; bake an additional 5 minutes, or until cheese melts. Serves 6 to 8.

Quick-Fix Recipes

Ravioli Lasagna
Denise Moloney, Brooksville, FL

1 lb. ground beef
1 onion, diced
26-oz. jar pasta sauce,
    divided
25-oz. pkg. frozen cheese
    ravioli, divided
1-1/2 c. shredded
    mozzarella cheese,
    divided

In a skillet over medium heat, brown beef with onion; drain. In a greased 11"x7" baking pan, layer one cup pasta sauce, half the frozen ravioli, half the beef mixture and half the cheese. Repeat layering with one cup pasta sauce and remaining ravioli and beef mixture. Add remaining pasta sauce. Bake, uncovered, at 425 degrees for 30 to 35 minutes. Top with remaining cheese and bake until melted, about 5 minutes. Serves 4 to 6.

Ravioli Lasagna

Easy Veggie Bake
Margie Schaffner, Altoona, IA

16-oz. pkg. frozen broccoli,
    carrots and cauliflower
8-oz. pkg. vegetable-
    flavored cream cheese,
    softened
10-3/4 oz. can cream of
    mushroom soup
1/2 to 1 c. seasoned
    croutons

Prepare vegetables according to package directions; drain and place in a large mixing bowl. Stir in soup and cream cheese; mix well. Spread into a greased one-quart casserole dish; sprinkle with croutons. Bake, uncovered, at 375 degrees until bubbly, about 25 minutes. Makes 4 to 6 servings.

Potato-Beef Casserole
Nancy Garrison, Jerseyville, IL

5 potatoes, peeled and
    diced
1 onion, diced
1/2 lb. ground beef,
    browned and drained
10-3/4 oz. can cream of
    mushroom soup

Place potatoes and onion in an ungreased 13"x9" baking pan; set aside. Mix ground beef and soup together; add one cup water. Spread over potatoes; bake at 350 degrees for one hour. Serves 6.

Quick tip
Cut leftover meatloaf into thick slices, wrap individually and freeze. Slices can be thawed and rewarmed quickly for scrumptious meatloaf sandwiches at a moment's notice.

Easy Veggie Bake

Double-Cheese Burritos

Double-Cheese Burritos

Jan O'Brien, Oakton, VA

4 to 5 boneless, skinless chicken breasts, cooked and shredded
8-oz. pkg. cream cheese, softened
12-oz. jar salsa, divided
8 10-inch flour tortillas
8-oz. pkg. pasteurized process cheese spread, cubed

Stir chicken, cream cheese and one cup salsa together; mix well. Spoon mixture down the center of each tortilla; roll up and place seam-side down in an ungreased 13"x9" baking pan. Set aside. Melt cheese cubes in a heavy saucepan; pour over tortillas. Spread with remaining salsa; bake at 350 degrees for 30 minutes. Makes 8 servings.

Pecan-Topped Sweet Potato Bake

Mary Coglianese, Kailua, HI

3 c. sweet potatoes, boiled, peeled and mashed
1/2 c. sugar
1/2 c. butter
2 eggs, beaten
1 t. vanilla extract
1/3 c. milk

Combine all ingredients; mix until very smooth and spread in a lightly greased 11"x7" baking pan. Sprinkle topping over potato mixture and bake, uncovered, for 25 minutes at 350 degrees. Serve hot. Makes 4 to 6 servings.

Topping:

1/3 c. butter, melted
1 c. brown sugar, packed
1/2 c. all-purpose flour
1 c. chopped pecans

Combine all ingredients in a bowl; mix well.

Hunter's Pie

Heidi Maurer, Garrett, IN

1 lb. roast beef, cooked and cubed
8-oz. can sliced carrots, drained
8-oz. can green beans, drained
12-oz. jar beef gravy
9-inch deep-dish pie crust, baked
11-oz. tube refrigerated bread sticks

Combine all ingredients except pie crust and bread sticks; spread into pie crust. Arrange unbaked bread sticks on top, criss-cross style. Bake at 350 degrees for 20 minutes, or until heated through and bread sticks are golden. Serves 4.

Quick tip

Even a quick supper can be memorable when it's thoughtfully served. Use the good china, set out cloth napkins and a jar of fresh flowers...after all, who's more special than your family?.

Reuben Casserole

JoAnn

6 slices rye bread, cubed
16-oz. can sauerkraut, drained and rinsed
1 lb. sliced deli corned beef, cut into strips
3/4 c. Thousand Island salad dressing
2 c. shredded Swiss cheese

Arrange bread cubes in a greased 13"x9" baking pan; cover with sauerkraut. Layer corned beef over sauerkraut; drizzle salad dressing over top. Cover with aluminum foil and bake at 400 degrees for 20 minutes. Remove foil; sprinkle with cheese and bake, uncovered, for another 10 minutes, or until cheese is melted and bubbly. Serves 6.

Reuben Casserole

Easy Gumbo Meatballs

Brenda Flowers, Olney, IL

2 lbs. ground beef
4 slices bread, crumbled
3/4 c. evaporated milk
10-3/4 oz. can chicken gumbo soup
10-1/2 oz. can French onion soup

Combine first 3 ingredients; form into one-inch balls. Arrange in an ungreased 13"x9" baking pan; pour soups on top. Bake at 350 degrees for 1-1/2 hours. Serves 6.

Cheesy Fiesta Bake

Brittany Trotter-McDowell, Ellsinore, MO

2 lbs. ground beef, browned and drained
1-1/4 oz. pkg. taco seasoning mix
2 8-oz. tubes refrigerated crescent rolls
16-oz. jar pasteurized process cheese sauce
4-oz. can diced green chiles

Combine ground beef and taco seasoning; set aside. Press one tube crescent rolls to cover the bottom of a lightly greased 13"x9" baking pan. Layer beef mixture and pasteurized process cheese sauce on top; sprinkle with green chiles. Arrange remaining package of crescent rolls on top; bake at 400 degrees for 25 to 30 minutes. Makes 8 servings.

Easy Gumbo Meatballs

Cheeseburger & Fries Casserole

Cheeseburger & Fries Casserole

Shari Miller, Hobart, IN

2 lbs. ground beef,
  browned and drained
10-3/4 oz. can golden
  mushroom soup

10-3/4 oz. can Cheddar
  cheese soup
20-oz. pkg. frozen
  crinkle-cut French fries

Combine ground beef and soups; spread in a greased
13"x9" baking pan. Arrange French fries on top. Bake,
uncovered, at 350 degrees for 50 to 55 minutes, or until
fries are golden. Makes 6 to 8 servings.

Chicken Kiev Casserole

John Alexander, New Britain, CT

12-oz. pkg. wide egg
  noodles, uncooked
1/4 c. butter, softened
1 t. garlic powder
1 T. fresh parsley, chopped
1 deli roast chicken, cubed,
  divided and juices
  reserved

2 c. frozen peas, thawed
1 c. whipping cream
paprika to taste
Optional: additional fresh
  parsley

Cook noodles according to package directions until just
tender; drain and set aside. In a bowl, combine butter,
garlic powder and parsley. Use one teaspoon of butter
mixture to grease a 13"x9" baking pan. Layer half the
chicken, half the noodles and all the peas; dot with
half the remaining butter mixture. Repeat layers with
remaining chicken, noodles and butter mixture. Pour
reserved chicken juices and cream over top; sprinkle
with paprika. Bake, uncovered, at 350 degrees for 30
minutes, or until hot and bubbly. Sprinkle with parsley,
if using. Serves 6.

Chicken Kiev Casserole

Quick tip

No-mess stuffed pasta shells! Spoon cheese
filling into a plastic zipping bag. Clip off a
corner of the bag and squeeze the filling into
shells, then toss away the bag.

Chicken-Broccoli Divan

Russian Chicken
Betty Richer, Grand Junction, CO

3 to 4 lbs. chicken
1/4 c. mayonnaise
1-1/2 oz. pkg. onion soup
  mix

1/2 c. Russian dressing
1 c. apricot preserves

Arrange chicken in an ungreased 13"x9" baking pan; set aside. Mix remaining ingredients; spread over chicken. Bake at 350 degrees for 1-1/4 hours. Serves 4.

Chicken & Stuffing Casserole
Sandy Tolbert, Big Stone Gap, VA

4 boneless, skinless
  chicken breasts, cooked
  and broth reserved
12-oz. pkg. stuffing mix
1/2 c. butter, melted

10-3/4 oz. can cream of
  mushroom soup
10-3/4 oz. can cream of
  chicken soup

Cool chicken; slice into cubes and set aside. Mix stuffing with butter; set aside. Whisk cream of mushroom soup and 1-1/4 cups of reserved broth together; set aside. Repeat with cream of chicken soup; set aside. Layer a third of the stuffing mixture in a lightly buttered 2-quart casserole dish; continue layering with half the chicken, mushroom soup mixture, another third of stuffing, the remaining chicken, the cream of chicken soup mixture. Top with remaining stuffing. Bake, uncovered, at 350 degrees for 30 to 45 minutes. Makes 4 servings.

Chicken-Broccoli Divan
Tiffany Mayberry, Harriman, TN

2 c. cooked chicken, cubed
16-oz. pkg. frozen broccoli
  flowerets, thawed
2 10-3/4 oz. cans cream of
  chicken soup

3/4 c. mayonnaise
1 t. lemon juice
1/2 c. shredded Cheddar
  cheese

Place chicken in a greased 13"x9" baking pan. Layer broccoli on top. In a bowl, stir together soup, mayonnaise and lemon juice. Pour soup mixture over broccoli; top with cheese. Bake, uncovered, at 350 degrees for 45 minutes, or until bubbly. Serves 4.

Quick tip

Dress up tube biscuits by brushing the tops of each biscuit lightly with beaten egg and arranging a fresh parsley leaf on each. Lightly brush again with egg and bake as directed.

Russian Chicken

Pot Roast Casserole

Sandy Rowe, Bellevue, OH

8-oz. pkg. fine egg noodles, cooked

2 c. beef pot roast, cooked and chopped

2 c. Alfredo sauce

1 c. sliced mushrooms

1/4 c. dry bread crumbs

Mix noodles, pot roast, Alfredo sauce and mushrooms in an ungreased 2-quart casserole dish; sprinkle with bread crumbs. Bake at 350 degrees for 20 to 30 minutes, until crumbs are golden. Serves 4.

Quick tip

A side dish time-saver. Purchase packaged mashed potatoes at the grocery store. Heat up, blend in sour cream and cream cheese to taste, then heat up again until well blended.

Pot Roast Casserole

Quick Salisbury Steak

French Rice
Michelle Lockett, Lebam, WA

1 c. long-cooking rice, uncooked
4-oz. can sliced mushrooms, drained
1/2 c. onion, chopped
10-1/2 oz. can French onion soup

1 c. beef consommé
1/2 c. butter, melted
1/3 c. water
1 T. fresh parsley, chopped
1 clove garlic, minced

Combine all ingredients in a lightly greased 2-quart casserole dish. Stir gently. Cover and bake at 350 degrees for 35 minutes, or until liquid is absorbed and rice is tender. Makes 4 to 5 servings.

Quick Salisbury Steak
Alma Meyers, Guernsey, WY

1 lb. ground beef
1-1/2 oz. pkg. dry onion soup mix

2 eggs, beaten
2 10-3/4 oz. cans golden mushroom soup

In a large mixing bowl, combine ground beef, soup mix and eggs; form into 4 patties. Place patties in an ungreased 13"x9" baking pan. Cover with soup. Bake at 350 degrees for 35 minutes. Makes 4 servings.

Speedy Spanish Rice

Jocelyn Medina, Phoenixville, PA

1 c. long-cooking rice, uncooked
1/2 c. onion, chopped
2 T. oil
2 c. chicken broth
5-1/2 oz. can tomato juice
1/2 t. garlic powder
1/2 t. chili powder
1/2 t. ground cumin
1/3 c. fresh cilantro, chopped

In a skillet over medium heat, sauté rice and onion in oil until onion is crisp-tender. Add remaining ingredients except cilantro. Bring to a boil; reduce heat and cover. Simmer for 15 minutes, or until liquid is absorbed. Fluff rice with a fork; fold in cilantro. Serves 6.

Quick tip

Serve roasted corn on the cob with dinner...ready in only 4 minutes! Place husked ears of corn under a broiler until golden on all sides.

Speedy Spanish Rice

Tomato-Beef Noodle Bake

Carol Wingo, Henderson, TX

1 lb. ground beef
1 onion, chopped
10-oz. can diced tomatoes with green chiles
10-3/4 oz. can cream of mushroom soup
8-oz. pkg. fine egg noodles, cooked

Brown beef and onion in a skillet over medium heat; drain. Add remaining ingredients; place in an ungreased 2-quart casserole dish. Bake at 350 degrees for 20 to 25 minutes, until hot and bubbly. Serves 4.

Tomato-Beef Noodle Bake

Wild Chicken & Rice

Wild Chicken & Rice
Kimberly Lyons, Commerce, TX

2 6.2-oz. pkgs. instant wild rice

4 boneless, skinless chicken breasts, chopped

3 c. water

10-3/4 oz. can cream of mushroom soup

8-oz. pkg. frozen mixed vegetables, thawed

Gently stir all the ingredients together. Spread into an ungreased 13"x9" baking pan. Bake, covered, at 350 degrees until juices run clear when chicken is pierced with a fork, about 45 minutes, stirring occasionally. Serves 4.

20-Minute Veggie Bake
Janice Lewis, Mansfield, OH

8-oz. pkg. elbow macaroni, cooked

1 onion, chopped

1/2 c. celery, chopped

1 green pepper, chopped

8-oz. can sliced mushrooms, drained

1/4 c. oil

garlic salt to taste

1 t. salt

1/4 t. pepper

1/2 c. green olives with pimentos, chopped

6-oz. can tomato paste

1 c. water

1/2 c. grated Parmesan cheese

Place macaroni in a lightly greased 2-quart casserole dish; set aside. In a skillet, sauté onion, celery, green pepper and mushrooms in oil until tender. Add seasonings, olives, tomato paste and water; simmer for 10 minutes. Pour over macaroni; top with cheese. Bake at 375 degrees for 20 minutes. Serves 4 to 6.

Baked Chiles Rellenos
Jean Edwards, Citrus Heights, CA

7-oz. can whole green chiles, drained

1/2 lb. sharp Cheddar cheese

2 eggs

1/2 c. all-purpose flour

1-1/2 c. milk

Slice chiles down the center; arrange in a lightly buttered 13"x9" baking pan and set aside. Slice cheese to fit inside chiles; place in chiles. Whisk eggs, flour and milk together; pour over chiles. Bake at 350 degrees for 45 to 50 minutes. Serves 4.

Baked Chiles Rellenos

Ranchero Macaroni Bake

Sharon Crider, Lebanon, MO

26-oz. can cream of
  mushroom soup
1 c. milk
6 c. cooked elbow
  macaroni

3 c. shredded Cheddar
  cheese
1 c. salsa
1 c. tortilla chips, coarsely
  crushed

In a large bowl, combine soup and milk. Stir in macaroni,
cheese and salsa. Spoon into an ungreased 3-quart
casserole dish. Bake at 400 degrees for 20 minutes. Stir;
sprinkle with tortilla chips. Bake an additional 5 minutes,
or until bubbly. Serves 8.

Classic Green Bean Casserole

Reggie Westhoff, Monticello, MO

4 14-1/2 oz. cans green
  beans, drained
2 10-3/4 oz. cans cream of
  mushroom soup

1/3 c. milk
6-oz. can French fried
  onions

Mix beans, soup and milk together; spoon into an
ungreased 13"x9" baking pan. Sprinkle with onions; bake
at 350 degrees for 45 minutes. Serves 8 to 10.

Green Chile Rice

Debbie Wilson, Weatherford, TX

3 c. cooked rice
12-oz. pkg. shredded
  mozzarella cheese

2 c. sour cream
4-oz. can diced green
  chiles

Combine ingredients; pour into an ungreased
1-1/2 quart casserole dish. Mix well; bake at 400 degrees
until bubbly, about 20 minutes. Makes 6 servings.

Sweet Potato-Apple Bake

Joann Sklarsky, Johnstown, PA

29-oz. can sweet potatoes
21-oz. can apple pie filling

16-oz. can whole-berry
  cranberry sauce

Carefully fold ingredients together; spread into a
buttered 2-quart casserole dish. Bake at 350 degrees
until potatoes are heated, about 30 to 45 minutes.
Serves 4.

Quick tip

Cupcakes for dessert tonight? Frost them
quickly by dipping in frosting rather than
using a spatula.

Sweet Potato-Apple Bake

Speedy Ham & Beans

Speedy Ham & Beans

Julie Sibbersen, Portage, MI

1-1/3 c. cooked instant rice
14-oz. can green beans, drained
5-oz. can chopped ham
1/3 c. mayonnaise
1 t. chicken bouillon granules
1-1/3 c. boiling water
1 T. dried, minced onion
1/2 c. shredded Cheddar cheese

Combine rice, green beans, ham and mayonnaise in a lightly greased 11"x7" baking pan; set aside. Dissolve bouillon in water; pour over rice mixture. Sprinkle with minced onion and mix well. Bake at 400 degrees for 15 minutes; sprinkle with cheese and bake an additional 5 minutes, or until cheese is melted. Makes 4 to 6 servings.

Mom's Chicken Casserole

Samantha Fishkin, Lauderdale Lakes, FL

6-oz. pkg. rice pilaf mix
4 to 6 boneless, skinless chicken breasts
2 c. stewed tomatoes

Prepare rice pilaf according to package directions, cooking for just half the time. Transfer pilaf to a greased 13"x9" baking pan. Place chicken breasts over pilaf. Spoon tomatoes over chicken. Bake, covered with aluminum foil, at 350 degrees for one hour, or until chicken juices run clear and all liquid is absorbed. Serves 4 to 6.

Mom's Chicken Casserole

Quick tip

It's true...place an onion in the freezer for just 5 minutes before chopping for no tears!

Potato Puff Casserole

Dawn Henning, Hilliard, OH

1 lb. ground beef
10-3/4 oz. can cream of
 mushroom soup
3 14-1/2 oz. cans green
 beans, drained

12 slices pasteurized
 process cheese spread
16-oz. pkg. frozen potato
 puffs

In a skillet over medium heat, brown beef; drain and stir
in soup. Pour beef mixture into a greased 13"x9" baking
pan. Top with green beans and sliced cheese. Arrange
a single layer of potato puffs over cheese. Cover with
aluminum foil and bake at 400 degrees for 20 minutes,
or until cheese is melted. Uncover and bake again for
10 minutes, or until potato puffs are golden.
Serves 6 to 8.

Potato Puff Casserole

Hurry-Up Italian Casserole

Narita Roady, Pryor, OK

4 zucchini, thinly sliced
1/2 c. water
1 lb. ground beef
1/2 c. onion, chopped
2 cloves garlic, minced
1-1/2 t. Italian seasoning

1/2 t. salt
1 T. olive oil
2 c. fresh spinach, torn
1-1/2 c. marinara sauce
1-1/2 c. shredded
 mozzarella cheese

Place zucchini and water in a saucepan over medium
heat. Cook until tender, about 5 minutes; drain.
Meanwhile, in a skillet over medium heat, brown beef,
onion and garlic. Drain; sprinkle with seasonings. Spoon
into a 9"x9" glass baking pan and set aside. Add oil to
same skillet; add spinach and stir until wilted. Combine
spinach and zucchini; mix well and spread over beef
mixture. Spread marinara sauce over top; sprinkle with
cheese. Bake, uncovered, at 350 degrees for 20 minutes,
or until bubbly and cheese is melted. Makes 6 servings.

Salsa Lasagna

Lori Lybarger, Gambier, OH

16-oz. can refried beans
1 c. salsa
9 lasagna noodles, cooked
 and divided

1 c. cottage cheese, divided
1-1/2 c. shredded Cheddar
 cheese, divided

Combine refried beans and salsa in a small saucepan;
heat until warmed, stirring well. Spread 2 tablespoons
salsa mixture in the bottom of an ungreased 8"x8"
baking pan; arrange 3 noodles on top. Layer with half
the remaining salsa mixture, half the cottage cheese and
then 1/2 cup Cheddar cheese. Repeat layers beginning
with the noodles; top with remaining noodles and
Cheddar cheese. Bake at 350 degrees until bubbly, about
30 minutes. Makes 9 servings.

Hurry-Up Italian Casserole

Homesteader's Casserole

Broccoli-Chicken Casserole

Gladys Brehm, Quakertown, PA

10-3/4 oz. can cream of
  mushroom soup
1-1/2 c. milk
6-oz. pkg. chicken-flavored
  stuffing mix
3 c. cooked chicken, cubed
10-oz. pkg. frozen chopped
  broccoli, thawed
1 onion, finely chopped
2 stalks celery, finely
  chopped
Optional: 1/2 c. shredded
  mozzarella cheese

Whisk soup and milk together in a large bowl. Stir in remaining ingredients except cheese; mix well. Transfer to a 3-quart casserole dish that has been sprayed with non-stick vegetable spray. Bake, uncovered, at 350 degrees for 35 to 40 minutes. If desired, sprinkle with cheese during the last 10 minutes of baking time. Serves 4 to 6.

Homesteader's Casserole

Roxanne Bixby, West Franklin, NH

9-oz. pkg. frozen green
  beans, thawed
8-oz. can small whole
  onions, drained
1 T. chopped pimento
1 lb. sausage links, cooked
3 c. instant mashed
  potatoes, cooked
1/2 lb. pasteurized process
  cheese spread, sliced

In a large mixing bowl, combine beans, onions and pimento. Layer half of the sausage, half of the potatoes and half the cheese in a 2-quart baking dish coated with non-stick vegetable spray. Layer on remaining potatoes, green bean mixture, remaining sausage and cheese. Bake, covered, at 350 degrees for 30 minutes. Makes 4 to 6 servings.

Country-Style Creamed Cabbage

Candra Graves, Mannford, OK

10 c. cabbage, chopped
Optional: 1/4 c. bacon
  drippings
10-3/4 oz. can cream of
  chicken soup
1/4 c. milk
8-oz. pkg. pasteurized
  process cheese spread,
  cubed
salt and pepper to taste

Place cabbage and bacon drippings, if using, in a large stockpot. Add enough water to cover. Cook over medium-high heat until tender, about 45 minutes to one hour, adding more water if needed. While cabbage is cooking, mix together remaining ingredients in a large bowl. Drain cabbage and add to soup mixture; mix well. Place in a greased 13"x9" baking pan. Bake, uncovered, at 350 degrees for 30 minutes, until bubbly and cheese has melted. Serves 8.

Quick tip

Just need a little something while dinner is baking? Slice up some fresh veggies and serve with this super-simple dip. Blend 1 cup sour cream, 1 cup cottage cheese, 1 packet dried vegetable soup mix and 1 finely sliced green onion.

Scalloped Chicken

Ellen Forney, Ravenna, OH

3 to 4 c. cooked chicken, chopped

10-3/4 oz. can cream of mushroom soup

2 c. round buttery crackers, crushed and divided

2 T. butter, melted

In a lightly greased 2-quart baking dish, combine chicken, soup and 1/2 cup crackers. Combine remaining crackers with butter and sprinkle over top of chicken mixture. Bake at 350 degrees for 40 minutes. Makes 4 to 6 servings.

Scalloped Chicken

Pork Chops & Rice

Caroline Trinidad, McAlester, OK

4 to 8 pork chops

1 to 2 T. oil

1-1/2 oz. pkg. onion soup mix

2 c. water

2 green peppers, sliced and divided

1 c. long-cooking rice, uncooked

Sauté pork chops in oil in a skillet until browned on both sides; remove to a platter. Add soup mix and water to same skillet; cook and stir until mix dissolves. Layer half the green peppers in an ungreased 13"x9" baking pan; sprinkle with rice. Arrange pork chops on top; pour soup mixture over the pork chops. Top with remaining peppers; cover and bake at 325 degrees for 45 minutes to one hour. Serves 4 to 8.

Quick tip

Over the weekend, prepare the week's salads ahead of time so tonight's dinner is quick & easy! Store salad in a slightly damp plastic zipping bag and refrigerate; it will be fresh for up to 4 days.

Pork Chops & Rice

Quick-Fix Recipes

Ham & Swiss Casserole

Lauren Klein, Savannah, GA

1 c. sour cream
12-oz. pkg. shredded Swiss
  cheese, divided
8-oz. pkg. elbow macaroni,
  cooked
3 c. cooked ham, chopped

In a small mixing bowl, combine sour cream and 3/4 of cheese. In a lightly greased 13"x9" baking pan, place macaroni and ham. Add sour cream mixture to baking pan; stir until blended. Top with remaining cheese. Bake, uncovered, at 350 degrees for 30 minutes or until bubbly. Makes 6 to 8 servings.

Rice & Monterey Jack Casserole

Michelle Serrano, Ramona, CA

2 c. sour cream
3 c. prepared rice
2-oz. can diced green
  chiles
1 c. shredded Monterey
  Jack cheese

Combine sour cream, rice and chiles; arrange in layers with cheese in an ungreased 1-1/2 quart casserole dish. Bake at 350 degrees until heated through, about 15 minutes. Makes 6 servings.

Ham & Swiss Casserole

Cornbread Corn Casserole

Cornbread Corn Casserole

Tina Knotts, Marysville, OH

8-1/2 oz. pkg. corn muffin
   mix
2 15-oz. cans creamed
   corn

1 egg
1/3 c. butter, melted
3/4 c. sour cream

Combine ingredients together; pour into a greased
13"x9" baking pan. Bake at 375 degrees for 35 to
45 minutes. Makes 15 to 18 servings.

Quick tip

Top slices of warm bread with flavorful
Basil-Tomato Butter...it's easy to make.
Blend 1/2 cup softened butter with 1/3 cup
shredded fresh basil, 1 tablespoon tomato
paste and 1/4 teaspoon salt..

Bermuda Pork & Rice

Anne DeGroff, Amsterdam, NY

2 to 4 thick boneless pork
  chops

salt and pepper to taste

1/2 red onion, thinly sliced

1 c. long-cooking rice,
  uncooked

29-oz. can whole tomatoes,
  chopped

1 c. water

Sprinkle pork chops to taste with salt and pepper; place in a greased 13"x9" baking pan. Top with onion slices, rice and tomatoes with their juice. Pour water over top; cover with aluminum foil. Bake at 325 degrees for 2-1/2 to 3 hours. Serves 2 to 4.

Potatoes & Sausage Au Gratin

Tracy Walters, Denver, PA

16-oz. jar pasteurized
  processed cheese sauce,
  melted

16-oz. container sour
  cream

6 to 8 potatoes, peeled,
  cooked and diced

4 links smoked sausage,
  cut into bite-size pieces

Mix together melted cheese sauce and sour cream in a large bowl; stir in potatoes and sausage. Pour into an ungreased 13"x9" baking pan. Bake at 350 degrees for 35 minutes, until hot and bubbly. Serves 6 to 8.

Chopstick Tuna

Anna McMaster, Portland, OR

10-3/4 oz. can cream of
  mushroom soup

5 T. water

3-oz. can chow mein
  noodles, divided

1/4 c. onion, chopped

6-oz. can tuna, drained

1/2 c. salted cashews,
  chopped

1 c. celery, chopped

In a medium bowl, combine soup and water. Add half the noodles and remaining ingredients. Toss well and place in an ungreased 11"x7" baking pan. Sprinkle remaining noodles on top. Bake at 375 degrees for 15 minutes, or until hot and bubbly. Serves 4 to 6.

Quick tip

Boneless chicken breasts cook up quickly and evenly when flattened. Simply place chicken between two pieces of plastic wrap and gently pound to desired thickness with a meat mallet or a small skillet.

Chopstick Tuna

Creamy Salmon Manicotti

Creamy Salmon Manicotti
Cheri Maxwell, Gulf Breeze, FL

16-oz. container ricotta cheese

7.1-oz. pkg. boneless, skinless, pink salmon, flaked

1 egg, beaten

8 cooked manicotti shells

16-oz. jar Alfredo sauce

Garnish: dill weed

In a medium bowl, combine ricotta, salmon and egg until well mixed. Using a small spoon, fill each manicotti shell with the ricotta mixture; if there is any mixture left, stir into sauce. Place filled manicotti in a lightly greased 11"x7" baking pan. Pour sauce over manicotti. Sprinkle with dill. Bake covered at 350 degrees for 35 to 40 minutes. Serves 4 to 6.

Quick tip

Save chopping time...use a garlic press. Don't even bother peeling the clove, just place it in the garlic press and close. The peel slides right off and the paste is easily removed for any recipe.

Company Chicken
Jo Anne Hayon, Sheboygan, WI

8 slices Canadian bacon

4 boneless, skinless chicken breasts

10-3/4 oz. can cream of mushroom soup

1 c. sour cream

Garnish: green onions, chopped

Place bacon in the bottom of a greased 13"x9" baking pan; arrange chicken breasts on top. Bake at 350 degrees for 30 minutes. Combine soup and sour cream; spread over the chicken. Continue baking an additional 30 minutes. Garnish with onions. Serves 4.

Pizza Mac & Cheese
Jesse Ireland, St. Augustine, FL

7-1/4 oz. pkg. macaroni & cheese

2 eggs, beaten

16-oz. jar pizza sauce

4-oz. pkg. sliced pepperoni

1 c. shredded mozzarella cheese

Prepare macaroni and cheese according to package directions; remove from heat. Add eggs; mix well. Pour into a greased 13"x9" baking pan; bake at 375 degrees for 10 minutes. Spread with pizza sauce; layer pepperoni and mozzarella cheese on top. Return to oven until cheese melts, about 10 minutes. Makes 8 servings.

Crunchy Corn Chip Chicken

Tegan Reeves, Auburndale, FL

6 boneless, skinless
chicken breasts

10-3/4 oz. can cream of
chicken soup

2 c. shredded Cheddar
cheese, divided

1-1/4 oz. pkg. taco
seasoning mix

2 c. barbecue corn chips,
crushed

Arrange chicken in an ungreased 13"x9" baking pan; set aside. Combine soup, one cup cheese and taco seasoning together; spread over chicken. Bake at 450 degrees for 45 minutes; sprinkle with corn chips and remaining cheese. Return to oven; bake until cheese melts, about 5 minutes. Makes 6 servings.

Cheeseburger Bake

Jennifer Dutcher, Lewis Center, OH

8-oz. tube refrigerated
crescent rolls

1 lb. ground beef, browned
and drained

15-oz. can tomato sauce

1-1/4 oz. pkg. taco
seasoning mix

2 c. shredded Cheddar
cheese

Unroll crescent roll dough; press into a greased 9" round baking pan, pinching seams closed. Bake at 350 degrees for 10 minutes; set aside. Add beef, seasoning and tomato sauce to a skillet; heat through, about 7 minutes. Pour into crust; sprinkle cheese on top. Bake for 10 to 15 minutes. Set aside 5 minutes before serving. Serves 4.

Quick Pizza Casserole

Michelle Wittenberg, Long Beach, CA

6-oz. pkg. shell macaroni,
cooked

8-oz. jar pizza sauce

8-oz. container cottage
cheese

4-oz. pkg. shredded
mozzarella cheese

4-oz. pkg. sliced
pepperoni, halved

1/2 c. onion, chopped

1/2 t. dried basil

1 T. grated Parmesan
cheese

In a 2-quart microwave-safe dish, combine all ingredients except Parmesan cheese; blend well. Sprinkle Parmesan cheese over top. Cover and microwave on high for 7 to 9 minutes. Makes 4 to 6 servings.

Quick tip

Smoked sausage links are a great choice for weeknight meals...just brown and serve. Different flavors like hickory-smoked or cheese-filled can really jazz up a recipe. Be sure to select fully-cooked sausages, not the uncooked kind. .

Quick Pizza Casserole

Chicken & Biscuit Bake

Chicken & Biscuit Bake

Beverly Krosch, Elmore, MN

12-oz. tube refrigerated
  buttermilk biscuits
12-1/2 oz. can chicken
1/2 c. milk

10-3/4 oz. can cream of
  chicken soup
4 slices American cheese

Arrange biscuits in a greased 9"x9" baking pan; set aside. Mix chicken, milk and soup together; pour over biscuits. Bake at 350 degrees for 25 minutes; place cheese slices on top and return to oven until cheese melts. Serves 4.

Hearty Beef Stew

Nadine Thomas, Valley Forge, PA

10-1/2 oz. can French
  onion soup
10-3/4 oz. can tomato soup
1 lb. stew beef cubes

5 to 6 redskin potatoes,
  quartered
1 c. baby carrots

Combine ingredients together; pour into an ungreased 13"x9" baking pan. Cover with aluminum foil; bake at 350 degrees for 1-1/2 to 2 hours. Serves 4 to 5.

Creamed Spinach Casserole

Leah Dodson, Covington, KY

2 10-oz. pkgs. frozen
  chopped spinach, thawed
  and drained
8-oz. pkg. cream cheese,
  softened

1/4 c. milk
salt and pepper to taste
1/3 c. seasoned croutons,
  crushed

Mix together all ingredients except croutons. Spoon mixture into an ungreased one-quart casserole dish. Sprinkle with croutons. Bake at 350 degrees for 25 to 30 minutes, or until heated through. Serves 6.

Quick tip

Bouillon cubes are an easy substitute for canned chicken and beef broth. To make one cup of broth, dissolve a bouillon cube in one cup of boiling water. Use 1-3/4 cups prepared bouillon to replace a 14-ounce can of broth.

Quick & Easy Parmesan Asparagus

Paula Smith, Ottawa, IL

4 lbs. asparagus, trimmed
1/4 c. butter, melted
2 c. shredded Parmesan
  cheese
1 t. salt
1/2 t. pepper

In a large skillet, add asparagus and one inch of water. Bring to a boil. Reduce heat; cover and simmer for 5 to 7 minutes, until crisp-tender. Drain and arrange asparagus in a greased 13"x9" baking pan. Drizzle with butter; sprinkle with Parmesan cheese, salt and pepper. Bake, uncovered, at 350 degrees for 10 to 15 minutes, until cheese is melted. Serves 8 to 10.

Baked French Onion Rice

Tammie McClendon, Guild, TN

1 c. long-cooking rice,
  uncooked
14-1/2 oz. can beef broth
10-1/2 oz. can French
  onion soup
4-oz. can mushroom stems
  and pieces, drained
1/4 c. margarine

Place rice into an ungreased 2-quart casserole dish. Add beef broth, soup and mushroom pieces, stirring well. Dot with margarine; bake at 350 degrees for 50 minutes. Makes 4 servings.

Citrus Apple Sweet Potatoes

Carolyn Kent, Evant, TX

6 sweet potatoes, peeled,
  boiled and mashed
2 c. applesauce
1/2 c. brown sugar, packed
4 T. butter
1/2 c. orange juice

Mix ingredients together; place in a lightly buttered 2-quart casserole dish. Bake at 350 degrees for 40 minutes. Serves 8 to 10.

Quick tip

Stem and seed a green pepper in a flash...hold the pepper upright on a cutting board. Use a sharp knife to slice each of the sides from the pepper. You'll then have four large seedless pieces ready for slicing or chopping.

Quick & Easy Parmesan Asparagus

Quick-Fix Chicken Pot Pie

Quick-Fix Chicken Pot Pie

Ashley Causey, Lumberton, TX

1/2 c. plus 2 T. butter, divided
3 boneless skinless chicken breast, cubed
1 t. garlic powder
1 t. onion powder
1/2 t. dried parsley
1 c. carrots, peeled and thinly sliced
1 c. frozen peas, thawed
10-1/2 oz. can cream of chicken soup
salt and pepper to taste
1-1/2 c. biscuit baking mix
1 c. milk

Melt 2 tablespoons butter in a skillet over medium heat; add chicken. Sprinkle chicken with seasonings; sauté until golden and juices run clear. Transfer chicken to a greased 2-quart casserole dish; layer with carrots and peas. In a small bowl, mix soup, broth, salt and pepper; pour over vegetables. In a separate bowl, stir together biscuit mix and milk; spoon over top. Melt remaining butter and drizzle over top. Bake, uncovered, at 350 degrees for 35 to 45 minutes, until topping is firm and golden. Serves 4.

Quick tip

Kitchen shears are so handy! You'll find yourself using them again & again for snipping fresh herbs, cutting green onions, chopping canned tomatoes right in the can and opening packages. Just remember to wash them with soap and water after each use..

Saucy Pizza Casserole

Pat Mollohan, Parkersburg, WV

16-oz. pkg. elbow macaroni, cooked
3 14-oz. jars pizza sauce
8-oz. pkg. sliced pepperoni
8-oz. pkg. diced pepperoni
8-oz. pkg. shredded mozzarella cheese

Combine ingredients together; mix gently. Spread into an ungreased 2-quart casserole dish; bake at 350 degrees for 35 to 45 minutes. Serves 6.

Cabbage-Rice Casserole

Jean Gallant, New Bedford, MA

1 head cabbage, shredded
1 c. long-cooking rice, uncooked
2 c. water
2 lbs. ground beef, browned and drained
28-oz. jar spaghetti sauce

Place cabbage in a greased 13"x9" baking pan; spread rice on top. Pour water over rice; spoon beef over top. Pour sauce evenly over beef; bake, uncovered, at 375 degrees for 1-1/2 to 2 hours. Mix together before serving. Serves 6.

Simple Sides & Meatless Meals

Packed with plenty of flavor, these dishes are perfect alongside simple suppers, fancy dinners or special holiday meals. Budget-friendly and easy to make, veggie casseroles are a great way to stretch a meal to share with drop-in guests too!

Vegetarian Mexican Pie

Vegetarian Mexican Pie

Sonya Labbe, West Hollywood, CA

12 6-inch corn tortillas
1 c. black beans, drained and rinsed
1 c. red kidney beans, drained and rinsed
4-oz. can chopped green chiles
1-1/2 c. green or red salsa
1 c. sour cream
2 c. shredded Monterey Jack cheese

Layer 4 tortillas in a lightly greased 8"x8" baking pan, overlapping slightly. Top tortillas with 1/2 cup black beans, 1/2 cup kidney beans, 1/4 cup chiles, 1/2 cup salsa, 1/3 cup sour cream and 2/3 cup cheese. Add 4 more tortillas; repeat layering. Top with remaining tortillas, salsa, sour cream and cheese. Bake, uncovered, at 375 degrees, until bubbly and golden, 30 to 40 minutes. Makes 4 servings.

Creamy Asparagus Casserole

Angela Murphy, Tempe, AZ

15-oz. can asparagus spears, drained
10-3/4 oz. can cream of mushroom soup
1-1/2 c. cooked rice
1 onion, finely chopped
1 c. shredded Cheddar cheese

Combine all ingredients and place in a greased 11"x7" baking pan. Cover and bake at 325 degrees for 30 minutes. Serves 4 to 6.

Quick tip

Love a crunchy golden crumb topping on your mac & cheese? Toss some soft fresh bread crumbs with a little melted butter and sprinkle them on the unbaked casserole.

Cheesy Lentils & Rice Casserole

Shirley Howie, Foxboro, MA

3/4 c. dried lentils, uncooked
1/2 c. long-cooking rice, uncooked
3 c. chicken broth
2 T. dried, minced onion
1/2 t. dried basil
1/4 t. dried oregano
1/4 t. dried thyme
1/4 t. garlic powder
3/4 c. shredded Cheddar cheese

Blend all ingredients except cheese in a 2-quart casserole dish. Bake, covered, at 300 degrees for one hour and 15 minutes. Uncover and top with cheese; bake for 15 minutes, or until cheese is melted. Serves 4 to 6.

Cheesy Lentils & Rice Casserole

Pesto Polenta Lasagna

Lori Rosenberg, University Heights, OH

18-oz. tube polenta,
  sliced 1/4-inch thick
  and divided
1/4 c. basil pesto sauce,
  divided

1-1/4 c. marinara sauce,
  divided
1 c. shredded mozzarella
  cheese
1/4 c. pine nuts

In a greased 11"x7" baking pan, arrange half of polenta slices in a single layer. Spread half of pesto over polenta; spoon half of marinara sauce over pesto. Repeat layering, ending with marinara sauce. Bake, uncovered, at 375 degrees for 25 minutes. Remove from oven; top with cheese and pine nuts. Place pan under a preheated broiler; broil until cheese is melted and nuts are toasted. Makes 8 servings.

Quick tip

Make your own flavorful, nutritious vegetable broth...free! In a freezer container, save up veggie scraps and trimmings like carrot peels and celery leaves. When the container is full, place the veggies in a soup pot, add water to cover and simmer gently for 30 minutes. Strain and use to make soup or freeze in ice cube trays to add extra flavor to recipes.

Spaghetti Squash Monterey

Spaghetti Squash Monterey

Angie Venable, Delaware, OH

1 spaghetti squash, halved
  lengthwise and seeds
  removed
1 onion, chopped
1/4 c. butter

1/2 c. sour cream
salt and pepper to taste
2 c. shredded Monterey
  Jack cheese, divided
paprika to taste

Place squash halves cut-side down in a large saucepan; add 2 inches of water. Cover and boil 20 minutes over medium-high heat, until tender. Remove squash from water and let cool slightly. Use a fork to pull spaghetti-like strands from squash; place in a bowl and set aside. Meanwhile, in a small skillet over medium heat, sauté onion in butter until tender. Add onion mixture to squash strands along with sour cream, salt, pepper and one cup cheese. Stir to mix; transfer to a greased 2-quart casserole dish. Sprinkle with remaining cheese and paprika. Bake, uncovered, at 325 degrees for 30 minutes. Serves 6 to 8.

Pesto Polenta Lasagna

Cavatappi & Cheese with Broccoli

Cavatappi & Cheese with Broccoli
Stefanie St. Pierre, South Dennis, MA

1-1/2 c. cavatappi pasta, uncooked
4-1/2 T. butter, divided
4-1/2 T. all-purpose flour
1/4 t. dry mustard
3/4 t. salt
1/4 t. pepper
3 c. milk
3/4 t. Worcestershire sauce
1/4 c. onion, finely chopped
8-oz. pkg. shredded sharp Cheddar cheese
1/2 bunch broccoli, chopped
3 T. Italian-seasoned dry bread crumbs

Cook pasta according to package directions; drain. Transfer pasta to a lightly greased 2-quart casserole dish; set aside. In a saucepan over medium heat, melt 2 tablespoons butter; blend in flour, mustard, salt and pepper. Gradually add milk, stirring until thickened. Add Worcestershire sauce, onion and cheese; stir until cheese is melted. Pour cheese sauce over pasta and add broccoli. Stir well to combine. Melt remaining butter and toss with crumbs; sprinkle over top. Bake, uncovered, at 350 degrees for 30 minutes, or until hot and bubbly. Makes 4 to 6 servings.

Summertime Squash Casserole
Melissa Currie, Phoenix, AZ

2 lbs. yellow squash, sliced
1 c. shredded Cheddar cheese
1/2 c. cottage cheese
4 eggs, beaten
3 T. butter, melted
3/4 c. dry bread crumbs
1 T. fresh parsley, chopped
1 t. salt
1/2 t. pepper

Simmer squash in a stockpot of water over medium-low heat until tender, 5 to 10 minutes; drain. Mix all ingredients together, adding the squash last. Pour into an ungreased 13"x9" baking pan. Bake at 350 degrees for 45 minutes. Serves 6 to 8.

Vegetable Patch Pot Pie
Megan Brooks, Antioch, TN

1 onion, chopped
8-oz. pkg. sliced mushrooms
1 clove garlic, minced
2 T. olive oil
2 carrots, peeled and diced
2 potatoes, peeled and diced
2 stalks celery, sliced
2 c. cauliflower flowerets
1 c. green beans, trimmed and snapped into 1/2-inch pieces
3 c. vegetable broth
1 t. kosher salt
1 t. pepper
2 T. cornstarch
2 T. soy sauce
1/4 c. water
2 9-inch pie crusts

In a skillet over medium heat, cook onion, mushrooms and garlic in oil for 3 to 5 minutes. Stir frequently. Stir in remaining vegetables and broth. Bring to a boil; reduce heat and simmer. Cook until vegetables are just tender, about 5 minutes. Season with salt and pepper. In a small bowl, combine cornstarch, soy sauce and water. Mix until cornstarch has dissolved. Stir mixture into vegetables; simmer until sauce thickens. Roll out one crust and place in an ungreased 11"x7" baking pan. Spoon filling evenly over pastry. Roll out remaining crust and arrange over filling; crimp edges. Bake at 425 degrees for 30 minutes, or until crust is golden. Makes 6 servings.

Quick tip
Serve up a Southern-style vegetable plate for dinner. With two or three scrumptious veggie dishes and a basket of buttery cornbread, no one will even miss the meat.

Simple Sides & Meatless Meals

Parmesan Scalloped Potatoes

Tina Goodpasture, Meadowview, VA

2 lbs. Yukon Gold potatoes,
  thinly sliced

3 c. whipping cream

1/4 c. fresh parsley,
  chopped

2 cloves garlic, chopped

1-1/2 t. salt

1/4 t. pepper

1/3 c. grated Parmesan
  cheese

Layer potatoes in a lightly greased 13"x9" baking pan. In
a bowl, stir together remaining ingredients except cheese;
pour over potatoes. Bake, uncovered, at 400 degrees
for 30 minutes, stirring gently every 10 minutes. Sprinkle
with cheese; bake again for about 15 minutes, or until
bubbly and golden. Let stand 10 minutes before
serving. Serves 8.

Shoepeg & Green Bean Casserole,

Kathie McWherter, Bentonville, AR

15-oz. can shoepeg corn,
  drained

14-1/2 oz. can green beans,
  drained

10-3/4 oz. can cream
  of celery soup

1 c. sour cream

1 c. shredded Cheddar
  cheese

1 c. round buttery
  crackers, crushed

1/2 c. butter, melted

Mix corn, green beans, soup, sour cream and cheese
together. Spread in a greased 2-quart casserole dish.
Top with cracker crumbs; drizzle butter over top. Bake,
uncovered, at 350 degrees for one hour, or until golden.
Makes 6 to 8 servings.

Parmesan Scalloped Potatoes

Cranberry-Apple Sweet Potatoes

Terri Melton, Taft, CA

21-oz. can apple pie filling

2 18-oz. cans sweet
  potatoes, drained and cut
  into bite-size pieces

8-oz. can whole-berry
  cranberry sauce

2 T. apricot preserves

2 T. orange marmalade

Spread pie filling in a lightly greased 8"x8" baking
pan. Arrange sweet potatoes on top. Mix remaining
ingredients; spoon over sweet potatoes. Bake, uncovered,
at 350 degrees for 20 to 25 minutes, until hot and bubbly.
Serves 6.

Cranberry-Apple Sweet Potatoes

Broccoli & Ricotta-Stuffed Shells

Broccoli & Ricotta-Stuffed Shells

Crystal Inestroza, Athens, AL

12-oz. pkg. jumbo pasta
  shells, uncooked

16-oz. container ricotta
  cheese

1/4 c. shredded Parmesan
  cheese

1 egg, beaten

1 T. garlic, minced

1 t. Italian seasoning

1/4 t. pepper

10-oz. pkg. frozen chopped
  broccoli, thawed and
  well drained

2 15-oz. jars Alfredo sauce

1 c. water

Cook pasta according to package directions. Drain
and rinse with cold water. Meanwhile, in a bowl, mix
remaining ingredients except sauce and water. Stuff
each shell with one tablespoon of ricotta mixture.
Arrange shells in a lightly greased 13"x9" baking pan;
set aside. Combine sauce and water in a saucepan; heat
over medium-low heat until warmed through. Ladle
sauce over shells, covering all shells with sauce. Reserve
any remaining sauce for another use. Cover pan with
aluminum foil. Bake at 350 degrees for 40 to 45 minutes,
until hot and bubbly. Serves 6.

Quick tip

Blanching makes fresh veggies like green beans
crisp and bright. Bring a large pot of salted water
to a rolling boil, add trimmed veggies and boil
for 3 to 4 minutes, just until they begin to soften.
Immediately remove veggies to a bowl of ice
water. Cool, drain and pat dry.

Sweet Potato Casserole

Sweet Potato Casserole

Dawn Romero, Lewisville, TX

4 c. mashed sweet
  potatoes

1/3 c. plus 2 T. butter,
  melted and divided

2 T. sugar

2 eggs, beaten

1/2 c. milk

1/3 c. chopped pecans

1/3 c. sweetened flaked
  coconut

1/3 c. brown sugar, packed

2 T. all-purpose flour

In a large bowl, mix together sweet potatoes, 1/3 cup
butter and sugar. Stir in eggs and milk. Spoon mixture
into a lightly greased 2-quart casserole dish. In a
separate bowl, combine remaining butter and other
ingredients. Sprinkle mixture over sweet potatoes. Bake,
uncovered, at 325 degrees for one hour, or until heated
through and bubbly. Serves 4.

Fabulous Baked Potato Casserole
Ginia Johnston, Greeneville, TN

6 to 7 potatoes, peeled and cubed

2 c. shredded Cheddar cheese

1 c. mayonnaise

1/2 c. sour cream

1 onion, diced

6 slices bacon, crisply cooked and crumbled

In a large saucepan, boil potatoes in water until fork-tender, about 20 minutes; drain and set aside to cool. Combine cheese, mayonnaise, sour cream and onion; mix in potatoes, tossing gently to coat. Spread potato mixture in a buttered 13"x9" baking pan; sprinkle bacon on top. Bake, uncovered, at 350 degrees until golden and bubbly, about 20 to 25 minutes. Serves 8.

Fabulous Baked Potato Casserole

Pinto Bean Dinner
Moriah Clark, Butler, OH

9-oz. pkg. tortilla chips, crushed

2 30-oz. cans pinto beans, drained and rinsed

15-oz. corn, drained

14-1/2 oz. can petite diced tomatoes, drained

8-oz. can tomato sauce

1-1/4 oz. pkg. taco seasoning mix, or more to taste

2 c. shredded Cheddar cheese

Garnish: sour cream, salsa, shredded lettuce, sliced black olives

Sprinkle crushed tortilla chips into a greased 13"x9" baking pan; set aside. In a large bowl, combine beans, corn, tomatoes, tomato sauce and taco seasoning; mix well. Spoon mixture over chips; sprinkle with cheese. Bake, uncovered, at 350 degrees for 20 to 25 minutes, until bubbly and heated through. Serve with desired toppings. Makes 8 servings.

Carrots Au Gratin
Faith Gregory, Hamilton, OH

2 c. carrots, peeled and thinly sliced

1/4 c. onions, minced

1/2 c. water

1/4 c. plus 3 T. butter, divided

1/4 c. all-purpose flour

1-1/2 c. milk

1/3 c. shredded Cheddar cheese

1 T. dried parsley

2 c. round buttery crackers, crushed

Cook carrots and onions in water until tender; drain. Add 1/4 cup butter and flour; stir in milk. Cook and stir until thickened. Remove from heat; add cheese and parsley. Pour into a greased 13"x9" baking pan; set aside. Mix remaining butter with cracker crumbs; sprinkle on top. Bake at 375 degrees for 20 minutes. Serves 4.

Carrots Au Gratin

Surprise Scalloped Corn

Surprise Scalloped Corn
Jana Temple, Colorado Springs, CO

14-3/4 oz. can creamed
  corn
15-oz. can corn, drained
1/4 c. butter, melted and
  slightly cooled
8-1/2 oz. pkg. corn muffin
  mix

2 eggs, beaten
1/4 c. sugar
8-oz. container sour cream
1 c. shredded Cheddar
  cheese

In a large bowl, mix together all ingredients. Spoon into a greased 3-quart casserole dish. Batter will rise slightly during baking, so make sure there is 1/2 to one-inch space in dish above batter. Bake, uncovered, at 350 degrees for 50 to 60 minutes, until golden. Serves 4 to 6.

Family-Favorite Corn Soufflé
Donna Maltman, Toledo, OH

15-oz. can corn, drained
8-1/2 oz. pkg. cornbread
  mix
14-3/4 oz. can creamed
  corn

1 c. sour cream
1/4 c. butter, melted
8-oz. pkg. shredded
  Cheddar cheese

Combine all ingredients except cheese. Pour into a lightly greased 13"x9" baking pan. Cover with aluminum foil. Bake at 350 degrees for 30 minutes. Uncover; top with cheese. Return to oven and continue baking until cheese is bubbly and golden, about 15 minutes. Serves 8 to 10.

Family-Favorite Corn Soufflé

Herbed Corn Bake
Nikole Morningstar, Norfolk, VA

1/4 c. butter
1/2 c. cream cheese,
  softened
1/4 t. onion salt

1 T. fresh chives, chopped
10-oz. pkg. frozen corn,
  thawed

Melt butter in a heavy saucepan over low heat. Add cream cheese, onion salt and chives, stirring until cheese melts. Add corn; mix well. Spoon into an ungreased 1-1/2 quart casserole dish. Cover and bake at 325 degrees until bubbly, about 45 minutes. Makes 4 servings.

Quick tip

A dollop of lemon butter adds flavor to plain steamed vegetables. Simply blend 2 tablespoons softened butter with the zest of one lemon.

Zucchini-Corn Casserole

Dani Simmers, Kendallville, IN

3 lbs. zucchini, cubed
2 c. fresh or frozen corn
1 onion, chopped
1 green pepper, chopped
2 T. butter
salt and pepper to taste
4 eggs, lightly beaten
1 c. shredded Cheddar cheese
paprika to taste

In a saucepan, cook zucchini in boiling water for 2 to 3 minutes; drain and set aside. In a skillet over medium heat, sauté corn, onion and green pepper in butter until crisp-tender. Remove from heat and add zucchini to corn mixture; season with salt and pepper and let cool slightly. Stir in eggs and transfer to a greased 13"x9" baking pan. Top with cheese and paprika. Bake, uncovered, at 350 degrees for 40 minutes, or until lightly golden and bubbly. Serves 6 to 8.

Zucchini-Corn Casserole

Easy Carrot Casserole

Wendy Bush, Morrill, NE

4 to 5 carrots, peeled and chopped
1 c. pasteurized process cheese spread, cubed
1/4 c. butter
1/2 onion, finely chopped
3/4 c. potato chips, crushed

In a medium saucepan, cook carrots in salted water about 12 minutes; drain. Stir in cheese, butter and onion. Place mixture into a 2-quart casserole dish coated with non-stick vegetable spray; top with potato chips. Bake, uncovered, at 350 degrees for 30 minutes. Makes 6 to 8 servings.

Farmers' Market Casserole

Brad Warner, Marengo, OH

15-oz. can French-style green beans, drained
15-oz. can green peas, drained
15-oz. can whole kernel corn, drained
10-oz. jar pearl onions, cooked
1/4 c. butter
3 T. all-purpose flour
1 c. whipping cream
1/2 c. shredded Cheddar cheese
salt and pepper to taste
1 t. dry mustard
1/4 t. Worcestershire sauce
grated Parmesan cheese to taste

Combine vegetables in a lightly greased 13"x9" baking pan. Melt butter in a saucepan over medium heat; stir in flour. Cook together until well blended. Gradually stir in cream and continue stirring until sauce is thickened. Add cheese, salt, pepper, mustard and Worcestershire sauce. Stir until cheese is melted; pour over vegetables. Sprinkle with Parmesan cheese. Cover and bake at 350 degrees for 20 to 30 minutes. Serves 6 to 8.

Easy Carrot Casserole

Cheesy Corn & Hominy Posole
Paul Shoup, Caseville, MI

1 onion, chopped
2 4-oz. cans chopped green chiles
10-3/4 oz. can cream of mushroom soup
3 c. shredded Cheddar cheese
2 15-1/2 oz. cans hominy, drained
2 15-oz. cans shoepeg corn, drained

Combine onion, chiles, soup and cheese in a large bowl. Add hominy and corn; mix well. Transfer to a 13"x9" baking pan sprayed with non-stick vegetable spray. Cover with aluminum foil. Place a pan of water on the rack beneath pan in oven. Bake at 350 degrees for 30 minutes, or until heated through and cheese is melted. Serves 6 to 8.

Marsha's Zucchini-Tomato Bake
Marsha Kent, Chapin, SC

4 zucchini, sliced 1/2-inch thick
4 tomatoes, cubed
1 T. olive oil
1/4 c. shredded Parmesan cheese
Herbes de Provence or dried thyme to taste

Arrange zucchini slices in a lightly greased 13"x9" baking pan; top with tomatoes. Drizzle tomatoes with olive oil; sprinkle with Parmesan cheese and herbs. Bake, uncovered, at 350 degrees for 35 to 45 minutes. Serves 4 to 6.

Marsha's Zucchini-Tomato Bake

Game-Day BBQ Onions

Cheryl Breeden, North Platte, NE

11-oz. pkg. mesquite
  barbecue-flavored potato
  chips, divided
2 10-3/4 oz. cans cream of
  chicken soup

1/2 c. milk
4 sweet onions, thinly sliced
  and divided
2 c. shredded sharp Cheddar
  cheese, divided

Crush 2 cups of potato chips; set aside. Whisk together soup and milk; set aside. Place half of onion slices in the bottom of a 13"x9" baking pan coated with non-stick vegetable spray. Spread uncrushed chips over onions; add one cup cheese and half of soup mixture. Repeat layering. Top with reserved crushed chips. Bake, uncovered, at 350 degrees for one hour. Serves 10.

Game-Day BBQ Onions

Baked Macaroni & Eggplant

JoAnn

8-oz. pkg. ziti pasta,
  uncooked
2 to 3 T. olive oil
1 eggplant, peeled and thinly
  sliced
26-oz. jar pasta sauce,
  divided

8-oz. pkg. shredded
  mozzarella cheese, divided
6 T. grated Parmesan cheese,
  divided

Cook pasta as package directs; drain. Meanwhile, heat oil in a large skillet over medium heat. Cook eggplant slices in oil, a few slices at a time, until golden on both sides. Drain eggplant on paper towels; keep warm. Combine pasta and sauce, reserving one cup sauce for top of casserole. In a lightly greased 2-quart casserole dish, layer half the pasta mixture, 3/4 cup mozzarella cheese, half the eggplant and 2 tablespoons Parmesan cheese; repeat layers. Top with reserved sauce and remaining cheeses. Bake, uncovered, at 425 degrees for 15 minutes, or until hot and bubbly. Serves 4 to 6.

Swiss Scalloped Potatoes

Shirley Howie, Foxboro, MA

6 c. new potatoes, thinly
  sliced and divided
1/2 c. onion, finely
  chopped and divided
2 c. shredded Swiss
  cheese, divided

salt and pepper to taste
1 T. beef bouillon granules
1 c. boiling water

In a greased shallow 1-1/2 quart casserole dish, layer half the potato slices, half the onion and half the cheese. Sprinkle lightly with salt and pepper; repeat layers. Stir bouillon into boiling water; pour over potatoes and cheese. Bake, uncovered, at 400 degrees for 45 to 50 minutes, until potatoes are tender and crust is golden. Let stand 5 minutes before serving. Serves 6.

Broccoli Supreme

Chili Rice
Sally Davison, Page, AZ

3 c. cooked rice

10-3/4 oz. can cream of celery soup

4-oz. can diced green chiles, or to taste

1 c. shredded Monterey Jack cheese

1 c. sour cream

Optional: dried chives

Combine all ingredients except chives. Transfer to a lightly greased 2-quart casserole dish. Bake, uncovered, at 350 degrees for 20 minutes. Garnish with chives, if desired. Serves 6 to 8.

Broccoli Supreme
Linda Belon, Wintersville, OH

1 egg, beaten

10-oz. pkg. frozen chopped broccoli, partially thawed and drained

8-1/2 oz. can creamed corn

1 T. onion, grated

1/4 t. salt

1/8 t. pepper

1 c. herb-flavored stuffing mix

3 T. butter, melted

In a bowl, combine egg, broccoli, corn, onion, salt and pepper. In a separate bowl, toss stuffing mix with butter. Stir 3/4 cup of stuffing mixture into egg mixture. Turn into an ungreased 8"x8" baking pan. Sprinkle with remaining stuffing mixture. Bake, uncovered, at 350 degrees for 35 to 40 minutes, until bubbly. Makes 6 to 8 servings.

Oniony Zucchini Bake
Pam Messner, Gibbon, MN

3 c. zucchini, thinly sliced

4 eggs, beaten

1 c. biscuit baking mix

1/2 c. oil

1/2 c. onion, chopped

1/2 c. grated Parmesan cheese

2 T. fresh parsley, chopped

1/2 t. seasoned salt

1/2 t. dried oregano

1/2 t. salt

1/4 t. pepper

Mix all ingredients together. Pour into a greased 13"x9" baking pan. Bake at 350 degrees for 30 minutes. Serves 6 to 8.

Quick tip

Keep a couple of favorite side dishes tucked away in the freezer. Pair with hot sandwiches or a deli roast chicken to put a hearty homestyle meal on the table in a hurry.

Chili Rice

Easy Cheesy Bowtie Pasta

Easy Cheesy Bowtie Pasta

Elissa Ducar, Denton, TX

1/4 c. butter
1/4 c. all-purpose flour
1-1/2 c. milk
28-oz. can whole Italian tomatoes, drained, chopped and 1-1/4 c. liquid reserved
salt and pepper to taste
16-oz. pkg. bowtie pasta, cooked
1-1/2 c. grated mozzarella cheese

1/2 c. crumbled Gorgonzola cheese
1/2 c. shredded fontina cheese
1-1/3 c. grated Romano cheese, divided
1/2 c. fresh parsley, finely chopped

Optional: 1/2 c. shredded Cheddar cheese

Melt butter over medium heat in a heavy saucepan. Add flour and whisk for 3 minutes. Add milk and reserved tomato juice gradually, whisking constantly. Bring to a boil. Stir in tomatoes, salt and pepper. Reduce heat to medium-low; let simmer for about 3 minutes, or until thickened. Set aside. Combine pasta, mozzarella, Gorgonzola, fontina, one cup Romano and parsley in a large bowl; stir in tomato mixture. Pour into a greased 4-quart casserole dish; sprinkle with remaining Romano cheese and Cheddar. Bake at 375 degrees for 30 to 35 minutes, until bubbly. Let stand for 10 minutes before serving. Serves 6.

Quick tip

Place a bunch of fresh parsley in the fridge in a water-filled tumbler covered with a plastic bag. It will keep its just-picked flavor for up to a week.

Black Bean Casserole

Black Bean Casserole

Tami Bowman, Marysville, OH

1/3 c. long-cooking brown rice, uncooked
1 c. vegetable broth
1 T. olive oil
1/3 c. onion, diced
1 zucchini, thinly sliced
1/2 c. sliced mushrooms
1/2 t. ground cumin
salt to taste

cayenne pepper to taste
15-oz. can black beans, drained and rinsed
4-oz. can diced green chiles, drained
1/3 c. carrots, peeled and shredded
2 c. shredded Swiss cheese, divided

Combine rice and vegetable broth in a saucepan and bring to a boil. Reduce heat to low; cover and simmer for 45 minutes. Set aside. Heat oil in a skillet over medium heat; sauté onion until tender. Stir in zucchini, mushrooms, cumin, salt and cayenne pepper. Cook and stir until zucchini is lightly golden. In a large bowl, mix rice, onion mixture, beans, chiles, carrots and one cup cheese. Pour into a greased 13"x9" baking pan; sprinkle with remaining cheese. Cover casserole loosely with aluminum foil. Bake at 350 degrees for 30 minutes. Uncover and continue baking 10 minutes, or until bubbly and lightly golden. Serves 6 to 8.

Pineapple Casserole

Lynn Filipowicz, Wilmington, NC

20-oz. can crushed
  pineapple

20-oz. can pineapple
  chunks, drained

2 c. shredded sharp
  Cheddar cheese

1/4 c. sugar

6 T. all-purpose flour

1 sleeve round buttery
  crackers, crushed

1/2 c. butter, melted

Optional: pineapple rings,
  maraschino cherries

Mix together all ingredients except crackers, butter and
optional ingredients in a greased 13"x9" baking pan. Top
with crackers; drizzle butter over top. Bake, uncovered,
at 350 degrees for about 30 minutes, or until heated
through and bubbly. Garnish with pineapple rings and
cherries, if desired. Serves 8.

Pineapple Casserole

Cashew-Topped Broccoli

Irene Robinson, Cincinnati, OH

2 10-oz. pkgs. frozen
  broccoli spears, thawed

10-3/4 oz. can cream of
  celery soup

1 c. salted cashews

1 t. dried, minced onion

1/2 c. shredded Monterey
  Jack cheese

Arrange broccoli spears in a greased 13"x9" baking pan.
Combine remaining ingredients in a bowl; spoon over
broccoli. Bake, uncovered, at 350 degrees for 30 minutes,
or until hot and bubbly. Serves 6.

Gardeners' Casserole

Kathy Fortune, Wooster, OH

1 head cauliflower,
  chopped

1 head broccoli, chopped

8 carrots, peeled and
  sliced 1-inch thick

1 t. fresh chives, minced

salt and pepper to taste

1 onion, chopped

1/2 c. butter

1/4 c. all-purpose flour

8-oz. container whipping
  cream

2 c. milk

8-oz. pkg. cream cheese,
  softened

1 c. shredded Cheddar
  cheese

1 c. seasoned croutons,
  crushed

Steam cauliflower, broccoli and carrots until
crisp-tender. Place vegetables in a lightly greased
13"x9" baking pan; sprinkle with chives, salt and pepper.
Set aside. In a saucepan over medium heat, sauté onion
in butter; gradually add flour, stirring constantly.
Stir in cream and milk; add cream cheese, stirring
constantly until thick and smooth. Pour cheese sauce
over vegetables and mix gently. Sprinkle with shredded
cheese and croutons. Bake at 325 degrees for 30 to 35
minutes. Serves 8.

Cashew-Topped Broccoli

Mom's Butternut Squash Bake

Mushroom & Barley Casserole

Anne Marie Verdiramo, Rochester, MN

3/4 c. quick-cooking
   barley, uncooked

1/2 c. onion, chopped

1/4 c. butter

4-oz. can sliced
   mushrooms

14-1/2 oz. can chicken
   broth

1/2 c. sliced almonds

In a saucepan, sauté barley and onion in butter until golden; spoon into a greased 1-1/2 quart casserole dish. Add undrained mushrooms and broth; mix well. Bake, covered, at 350 degrees for one hour and 15 minutes. Remove cover and sprinkle with almonds. Bake, uncovered, for an additional 15 minutes. Serves 4 to 6.

Mushroom & Barley Casserole

Mom's Butternut Squash Bake

Sue Ellen Crabb, Glendale, AZ

10-3/4 oz. can cream of
   chicken soup

1 c. sour cream

1 c. carrots, peeled and
   shredded

2 lbs. butternut squash,
   cooked and lightly
   mashed

1/4 c. onion, chopped

8-oz. pkg. herb-flavored
   stuffing mix

1/2 c. butter, melted

In a bowl, combine soup and sour cream; stir in carrots. Fold in squash and onion. Combine stuffing mix and butter; spread 1/2 of mixture in bottom of a lightly greased 3-quart casserole dish. Spoon in squash mixture. Top with remaining stuffing mix. Bake, uncovered, at 350 degrees for 25 to 30 minutes. Serves 6 to 8.

Quick tip

Freeze extra homemade chicken broth in ice cube trays for down-home flavor when cooking rice, pasta or potatoes.

Spinach Soufflé
Gloria Robertson, Midland, TX

10-oz. pkg. frozen, chopped spinach, thawed
3 T. all-purpose flour
3 eggs, beaten
1/2 t. salt
12-oz. container cottage cheese
1 c. shredded Cheddar cheese
1/4 c. butter, melted

In a large mixing bowl, combine spinach with flour; add eggs, salt, cottage cheese, Cheddar cheese and butter. Place in a greased 13"x9" baking pan. Bake, covered, at 375 degrees for 45 minutes. Uncover and bake an additional 15 minutes. Makes 6 servings.

Zesty Eggplant Parmesan
Joanna Nicoline-Haughey, Berwyn, PA

2 eggplants, halved lengthwise
24-oz. jar pasta sauce, divided
1/4 c. extra virgin olive oil
1/2 c. seasoned dry bread crumbs
1/2 c. grated Parmesan cheese, divided
pepper to taste
8-oz. pkg. shredded mozzarella cheese

Cut eggplants into 1/2-inch slices; set aside. Spread 1-1/2 cups pasta sauce in a lightly greased 13"x9" baking pan. Arrange eggplant slices over sauce, overlapping slices. Drizzle with olive oil. Sprinkle with bread crumbs and half of the Parmesan cheese; season with pepper. Top with remaining sauce and Parmesan cheese. Bake, uncovered, at 450 degrees for 45 minutes. Top with mozzarella cheese. Return to oven for 3 minutes, or until cheese is melted. Makes 6 servings.

Honey-Mustard Glazed Sweet Onions
Judy Henfey, Cibolo, TX

4 sweet onions, cut into 8 wedges each
2 T. butter, sliced
1 T. plus 1 t. red wine vinegar
1 T. country-style Dijon mustard
2 t. honey
1/4 t. paprika
1/4 t. salt
pepper to taste

Place onions in a lightly greased casserole dish; set aside. Melt butter in a small saucepan over low heat; stir in remaining ingredients. Pour mixture over onions and stir well to coat. Bake, uncovered, at 350 degrees for 30 minutes or until soft and glazed, stirring occasionally. Serve warm. Makes 6 to 8 servings.

Quick tip

Don't store tomatoes in the refrigerator, they'll quickly lose their "just-picked" taste. Keep them on a pantry shelf instead.

Spinach Soufflé

Nutty Noodle Bake

Nutty Noodle Bake

Shelley Turner, Boise, ID

3 T. olive oil
2/3 c. chopped walnuts
1 onion, thinly sliced
2 carrots, peeled and
   coarsely grated
1 bunch Swiss chard,
   chopped
1 clove garlic, minced
1/3 c. fresh parsley,
   minced
1/2 t. dried thyme
1/2 c. soy sauce
1 c. sour cream
salt to taste
3 c. egg noodles, cooked
2 c. shredded Monterey
   Jack cheese

Heat oil in a large skillet over medium heat; sauté walnuts until lightly golden. Remove with slotted spoon and set aside; stir in onion and carrots. Sauté until onion is tender; remove from skillet. Add chard, garlic, parsley and thyme; sauté until chard is soft. Mix together soy sauce and sour cream; add to chard mixture along with walnuts. Sprinkle with salt to taste; set aside. Place noodles in a greased 2-quart casserole dish. Spoon vegetable mixture over top; sprinkle with cheese. Bake at 400 degrees for 15 minutes, or until cheese is bubbly. Serves 6.

Herbed Veggie-Cheese Casserole

Jo Ann

10-oz. pkg. frozen green
   beans
10-oz. pkg. frozen broccoli
10-oz. pkg. frozen
   cauliflower
10-oz. jar pearl onions,
   drained
1 c. shredded Cheddar
   cheese
2 10-3/4 oz. cans cream of
   mushroom soup
6-oz. pkg. herb stuffing
   mix

Cook frozen vegetables separately, just until crisp-tender. Arrange drained vegetables in layers in a greased 13"x9" baking pan. Arrange onions around the outer edge. Sprinkle with cheese; pour soup over all. Bake at 350 degrees for 30 minutes. Remove from oven; sprinkle half the stuffing over the top, reserving the rest for another recipe. Bake for an additional 15 minutes. Serves 8.

Hearty Vegetable Pot Pie

Marian Buckley, Fontana, CA

1 head cauliflower, cut
   into flowerets
1 butternut squash, peeled
   and cut into 1-inch cubes
2 parsnips, peeled and cut
   into 1-inch pieces
1 c. baby carrots
1 red pepper, cut into
   1-inch pieces
2 T. olive oil
salt and pepper to taste
1 c. vegetable broth
1 T. cornstarch
2 T. dry bread crumbs
2 t. fresh thyme, snipped
2 t. fresh oregano, snipped
2 9-inch deep-dish pie
   crusts
2 T. grated Parmesan
   cheese, divided
1 egg, beaten
1 T. water

In a large bowl, combine vegetables, oil, salt and pepper; toss to mix. Spread on a lightly oiled 15"x10" jelly-roll pan. Bake, uncovered, at 450 degrees for 30 minutes, stirring halfway through. In a small saucepan over medium heat, stir together broth and cornstarch; bring to a boil. Reduce heat; cook and stir for one minute, until thickened. Return vegetables to bowl; toss gently with broth mixture, bread crumbs and herbs. Place one crust in a 9" deep-dish pie plate. Sprinkle crust with one tablespoon cheese; spoon in vegetable mixture. Sprinkle with remaining cheese. Add remaining crust; crimp edges and vent with a knife. Whisk egg and water together; brush over crust. Bake at 450 degrees for 15 minutes. Reduce heat to 425 degrees; bake an additional 30 minutes, until golden. Let stand for 10 minutes before slicing. Makes 6 servings.

Quick tip

Zip up an everyday salad by tossing in some finely chopped apples, raisins and walnut pieces. Add edible flowers too! Pesticide-free chive blossoms, nasturtiums and violets are all perfectly edible.

Meatless Spaghetti Pie

Meatless Spaghetti Pie

Vickie

7-oz. pkg. spaghetti, uncooked
1 c. cottage cheese
3 eggs, divided
1-1/2 t. salt
1/8 t. pepper
1 c. shredded sharp Cheddar cheese
2 T. grated Parmesan cheese
Garnish: warm pasta sauce

Cook spaghetti according to package directions; drain. In a bowl, gently mix spaghetti, cottage cheese, 2 beaten eggs, salt, pepper and Cheddar cheese. Transfer to a greased 9" deep-dish pie plate. Beat together remaining egg and Parmesan cheese; spread over top. Bake, uncovered, at 350 degrees for 45 to 55 minutes, until a knife tip inserted in the center comes out clean. Cut into wedges; spoon some sauce over each wedge. Serves 6 to 8.

Easy Cheesy Ratatouille

Easy Cheesy Ratatouille

Amy Butcher, Columbus, GA

1 eggplant, peeled and cut into 1-inch cubes
1 onion, diced
1 red pepper, diced
1 zucchini, cut into 1-inch cubes
1/4 c. sun-dried tomato vinaigrette
14-1/2 oz. can diced tomatoes
1/4 c. grated Parmesan cheese
1 c. shredded mozzarella cheese

Sauté vegetables with vinaigrette in a large oven-safe skillet over medium heat. Add tomatoes with juice; cook for 15 minutes. Sprinkle with cheeses. Bake, uncovered, at 350 degrees for 15 minutes, or until vegetables are tender. Serves 6 to 8.

Italian Zucchini Casserole

Jeanne Allen, Menomonee, WI

3 zucchini, sliced
3 T. olive oil, divided
1 onion, sliced
1 clove garlic, minced
28-oz. can diced tomatoes
1 T. fresh basil, minced
1-1/2 t. fresh oregano, minced
1/2 t. garlic salt
1/4 t. pepper
1-1/2 c. favorite-flavor stuffing mix
1/2 c. grated Parmesan cheese
3/4 c. shredded mozzarella cheese

In a skillet over medium heat, cook zucchini in one tablespoon oil for 5 to 6 minutes, or until tender. Drain and set aside. In the same skillet, sauté onion and garlic in remaining oil for one minute. Add tomatoes with juice, basil, oregano, garlic salt and pepper; simmer, uncovered, for 10 minutes. Remove from heat; gently stir in zucchini. Place in an ungreased 13"x9" inch baking pan. Top with stuffing mix; sprinkle with Parmesan cheese. Cover and bake at 350 degrees for 20 minutes. Uncover and sprinkle with mozzarella cheese. Return to the oven and continue baking 10 minutes, or until cheese is bubbly and golden. Makes 6 to 8 servings.

3-Cheese Herb Penne

Carol Doggett, Shawnee, KS

3 T. butter
2 cloves garlic, minced
1/4 c. all-purpose flour
1 t. dry mustard
1/4 t. nutmeg
3 c. milk
8-oz. pkg. shredded
    Cheddar cheese
1 c. shredded Monterey
    Jack cheese

1/4 c. grated Parmesan
    cheese
2 T. fresh herbs, finely
    chopped, such as parsley,
    dill, oregano and basil
1/2 t. salt
pepper to taste
16-oz. pkg. penne pasta,
    cooked

Melt butter in a skillet over medium heat. Add garlic; sauté one minute. Whisk in flour, mustard and nutmeg. Pour in milk; continue to whisk until smooth. Bring to a boil, stirring constantly. Reduce heat and simmer one minute. Combine cheeses; reserve 3/4 cup and set aside. Add remaining cheese to sauce, a little at a time, stirring until cheese melts. Add herbs and seasonings. Toss pasta with sauce; sprinkle with reserved cheese. Spoon into a lightly greased 13"x9" baking pan. Bake, covered, at 350 degrees for 10 to 15 minutes. Uncover and broil for one to 2 minutes, until golden and bubbly. Serves 4 to 6.

Kathy's Eggplant Parm

Kathy Williams, Delaware, OH

4 eggs, beaten
3 T. water
2 eggplants, peeled and
    sliced 1/4-inch thick
2 c. Italian-style dry bread
    crumbs

2 c. grated Parmesan
    cheese, divided
28-oz. jar chunky-style
    pasta sauce, divided
2 c. shredded mozzarella
    cheese

Whisk together eggs and water in a shallow bowl. Dip eggplant slices into egg mixture. Arrange slices in a single layer on a greased baking sheet; bake at 350 degrees for 25 minutes, or until tender. Set aside. Mix bread crumbs and 1/2 cup Parmesan cheese; set aside. Spread a small amount of sauce in an ungreased 13"x9" baking pan; layer half the eggplant, one cup sauce and one cup crumb mixture. Repeat layering. Cover with aluminum foil and bake for 45 minutes. Remove foil; sprinkle with mozzarella cheese. Bake, uncovered, for an additional 10 minutes. Serves 6 to 8.

Susan's Vegetable Lasagna

Susan Province, Strawberry Plains, TN

2 t. olive oil
6 c. vegetables, diced,
    such as zucchini, yellow
    squash, carrots, broccoli,
    red pepper, mushrooms
1 onion, diced
2 cloves garlic, minced
2 to 6 T. soy sauce or
    Worcestershire sauce
pepper to taste
1/2 t. dried basil

1/2 t. dried oregano
26-oz. jar marinara sauce,
    divided
9-oz. pkg. no-boil lasagna
    noodles, uncooked and
    divided
1 c. ricotta cheese
1 c. grated Parmesan
    cheese
1-1/2 c. shredded
    mozzarella cheese

Over medium-high heat, drizzle oil into a skillet. Add vegetables and onion; stir-fry until onion turns translucent. Add garlic and soy sauce or Worcestershire sauce; continue cooking until vegetables are tender. Season with pepper, basil and oregano. Spoon 1/2 cup sauce into an ungreased 13"x9" baking pan. Arrange 1/3 of the noodles on the bottom; spoon on half the ricotta cheese and half the Parmesan cheese. Top with half of the vegetables. Repeat again, ending with remaining noodles. Pour on the remaining sauce and sprinkle with mozzarella cheese. Bake, uncovered, at 350 degrees for 25 to 30 minutes. Serves 8.

Quick tip

To keep rice from becoming sticky, don't stir it after cooking, instead, gently fluff it with a fork. It works every time!

Kathy's Eggplant Parm

Acorn Squash Fruit Cups

Acorn Squash Fruit Cups
Janis Parr, Ontario, Canada

2 acorn squash, halved
  and seeds removed
1/4 t. salt
2 c. tart apples, cored and
  chopped
3/4 c. cranberries

1/4 c. sugar
1/4 c. brown sugar, packed
2 T. butter, melted
1/4 t. cinnamon
1/8 t. nutmeg

Place squash cut-side down in an ungreased 13"x9" baking pan. Add one inch of hot water to the pan. Bake, uncovered, at 350 degrees for 30 minutes. Drain water from pan; turn squash over so cut side is up. Sprinkle with salt. Combine remaining ingredients and spoon into squash. Bake, uncovered, for 40 to 50 minutes longer, or until squash is tender. Makes 4 servings.

Scalloped Apples

Scalloped Apples
Jacqueline Kurtz, Reading, PA

10 tart apples, cored,
  peeled and sliced
1/3 c. sugar
2 T. cornstarch

1/2 to 1 t. cinnamon
1/8 t. nutmeg
2 T. butter, cubed

Place apples in a microwave-safe 2-1/2 quart bowl lightly sprayed with non-stick vegetable spray; set aside. Combine sugar, cornstarch and spices; sprinkle over apples and toss to coat. Dot with butter. Cover and microwave on high setting for 15 minutes, or until apples are tender, stirring every 5 minutes. Serves 6.

Cheesy Cottage Potatoes
Marsha Baker, Pioneer, OH

10 russet potatoes
1 onion, chopped
8-oz. pkg. pasteurized
  process cheese, cubed
1 slice fresh bread, torn
  into bite-size pieces
1/2 t. salt

Optional: 2-oz. jar
  pimentos, drained
1/2 c. butter, melted and
  divided
1/4 c. milk
2 c. corn flake cereal,
  crushed

In a stockpot, cover unpeeled potatoes with water. Bring to a boil over high heat. Cook until tender, 15 to 20 minutes. Drain and cool; peel potatoes and cut into cubes. In a large bowl, combine potatoes, onion, cheese, bread, salt and pimentos, if using. Drizzle with 6 tablespoons butter. Spoon mixture into a lightly greased 2-1/2 quart casserole dish. Drizzle milk over top. In a small bowl, combine crushed cereal with remaining butter; spread evenly over potato mixture. Bake, uncovered, at 350 degrees for 35 to 45 minutes, until bubbly and topping is golden. If making ahead of time, do not add milk and topping until just before baking. Makes 8 servings.

Cheesy Chile Rice

Wendy Reaume, Ontario, Canada

2 c. water
2 c. instant rice, uncooked
16-oz. container sour cream
4-oz. can diced green chiles
3 c. shredded Cheddar cheese, divided

In a saucepan over medium-high heat, bring water to a boil. Stir in rice; remove from heat. Cover and let stand 5 minutes, until water is absorbed. In a large bowl, mix together rice, sour cream, chiles and 2 cups cheese. Spread in a greased 2-quart casserole dish; top with remaining cheese. Bake, uncovered, at 400 degrees for 30 minutes, or until cheese is melted and top is lightly golden. Makes 6 servings.

Cheesy Chili Rice

Triple Cheese Mac

Linda Duffy, Mashpee, MA

6 T. margarine
2 cloves garlic, pressed
1/4 c. all-purpose flour
3-1/2 c. milk
1 T. spicy mustard
salt and pepper to taste
1 c. shredded sharp Cheddar cheese
1/2 c. shredded American cheese
1/4 c. grated Parmesan cheese
16-oz. pkg. elbow macaroni, cooked
1/4 c. dry bread crumbs

In a saucepan over medium heat, whisk together margarine, garlic and flour. Stir in milk, mustard, salt and pepper to taste. Cook and stir until thickened and smooth. Add cheeses, blending well. Stir in macaroni. Transfer to a greased 13"x9" baking pan. Top with bread crumbs and bake, uncovered, at 350 degrees until golden, about 35 minutes. Makes 6 servings.

Crispy Green Bean Bake

Tanya Duke, Bethany, OK

6 T. margarine, melted and divided
3 T. all-purpose flour
1 t. sugar
1 t. onion powder
1 c. sour cream
salt and pepper to taste
3 16-oz. cans green beans, drained
2 c. shredded Cheddar cheese
2 c. crispy rice cereal, crushed

Combine 3 tablespoons margarine, flour, sugar, onion powder, sour cream, salt and pepper; mix well. Stir in green beans; spread in an ungreased 13"x9" baking pan. Sprinkle with cheese; set aside. Mix cereal with remaining margarine; crumble over cheese layer. Bake at 350 degrees for 35 minutes. Serves 6.

Crispy Green Bean Bake

Garden-Fresh Tortilla Bake

Garden-Fresh Tortilla Bake
Dianna Likens, Columbus, OH

2 T. oil
1 lb. zucchini, sliced
1 onion, chopped
1 green pepper, chopped
7-oz. can diced green chiles
4 eggs, hard-boiled, peeled and chopped

salt, pepper and ground cumin to taste
2 T. all-purpose flour
1 c. sour cream
6 6-inch corn tortillas, cut into 6 wedges each
3 c. shredded Cheddar cheese

Heat oil in a skillet over medium heat; add zucchini, onion and green pepper. Cook until vegetables are just tender, about 5 minutes. Remove from heat. Stir in chiles, eggs, salt, pepper and cumin; set aside. Blend flour into sour cream until smooth; set aside. Arrange tortilla wedges in an ungreased 2-quart casserole dish. Layer with half the vegetable mixture, half the sour cream mixture and half the cheese. Repeat layers. Bake, uncovered, at 350 degrees for 30 minutes or until bubbly. Serves 6.

Quick tip

Don't toss out the stalks when preparing fresh broccoli...they're good to eat too. Peel stalks with a potato peeler, then chop or dice and add to salads, stir-fries or casseroles.

Chestnut Stuffing
Vickie

1 lb. whole chestnuts
2 qts. water
1 onion, chopped
1 T. butter
2 apples, cored and chopped

3/4 c. soft bread, cubed
1 T. fresh parsley, chopped
1/2 t. dried thyme
1/4 t. pepper
1/4 c. chicken broth

Cut an X in the flat side of each chestnut using a knife point. Boil chestnuts in water for 15 to 25 minutes. Drain and cool. Peel chestnuts and cut into quarters. Set aside. In a skillet, combine onion and butter; sauté until tender. Add chestnuts and remaining ingredients, mixing well. Spoon into a greased 1-1/2 quart casserole dish. Bake, covered, at 350 degrees for 30 minutes. Uncover and bake an additional 15 to 25 minutes. Serves 6 to 8.

Fancy Sunday Squash Dish
Virginia Shugart, Calhoun, GA

2 lbs. yellow squash, chopped
1/2 c. onion, chopped
1/2 c. water
8-oz. container sour cream
salt and pepper to taste
1/4 t. dried basil

1 c. soft bread crumbs
1/2 c. butter, melted
1/2 c. shredded Cheddar cheese
1/2 t. paprika
6 slices bacon, crisply cooked and crumbled

In a saucepan over medium heat, cook squash and onion in water until tender; drain and mash. Combine squash mixture, sour cream and seasonings. Pour into a greased 13"x9" baking pan. Toss together bread crumbs, butter, cheese and paprika; sprinkle over squash mixture. Top with bacon. Bake, uncovered, at 300 degrees for 20 minutes, or until hot and golden. Serves 6.

Chapter 4

Delicious Dinners

Looking for the best pasta casserole? We've got it. Pork chops, ham, ground beef...got 'em. Chicken, lasagna, shrimp... we've got them too! No matter what you're in the mood to cook, we've got a delicious recipe just waiting for you to try.

Hamburger Bundles

Hamburger Bundles
Julie Whiteside, Queenstown, MD

10-3/4 oz. can cream of
  mushroom soup
1/4 c. milk
1 lb. ground beef

1 T. catsup
2 t. Worcestershire sauce
6-oz. pkg. stuffing mix,
  cooked

In a medium bowl, blend together soup and milk. In a large bowl, combine beef, catsup and Worcestershire sauce. Divide mixture and shape into 4 patties. Place 1/4 cup of stuffing onto each patty and draw sides up to make a ball. Place in an ungreased 13"x9" baking pan; cover with soup mixture. Bake, uncovered, at 350 degrees for 35 to 45 minutes. Makes 4 servings.

Beefy Shepherd's Pie
Kathryn Jones, Cheyenne, WY

1 lb. lean ground beef
1/2 c. onion, chopped
1/3 c. catsup
1/3 c. mild salsa

1 c. frozen mixed
  vegetables
2 c. mashed potatoes
2 T. butter, sliced

Brown beef and onion in a skillet over medium heat. Drain; spread in a greased 8"x8" glass baking pan. Layer catsup, salsa and frozen vegetables over beef mixture. Cover with mashed potatoes; dot potatoes with pats of butter. Bake, uncovered, at 400 degrees for 30 to 40 minutes, until bubbly and golden. Serves 4.

Beefy Shepherd's Pie

Quick tip
A clever way to crumble ground beef...use a potato masher right in the skillet.

3-Bean Bake
Brenda Doak, Delaware, OH

1 lb. ground beef
6 slices bacon, diced
1 onion, chopped
1 green pepper, chopped
1 T. white vinegar
1 T. mustard
1/2 c. catsup

1/2 c. brown sugar, packed
15-oz. can kidney beans,
  drained and rinsed
16-oz. can chili beans
15-oz. can pork & beans
6 slices American cheese
1 c. tortilla chips, crushed

Brown ground beef, bacon, onion and pepper in a large skillet over medium-high heat; drain. Pour into an ungreased 3-quart casserole dish. Add vinegar, mustard, catsup, brown sugar and beans; mix to blend. Bake at 375 degrees for 45 to 50 minutes; remove from oven and top with cheese and chips. Bake an additional 5 to 10 minutes, until cheese is melted and bubbly. Serves 6.

...o Casserole

... butter, sliced
... shredded Cheddar
... eese

...n in a 13"x9" baking
pan ... table spray. Dot with
butter; sprinkle with cheese. ...ke, uncovered, at
350 degrees for 1-1/2 hours, or until potatoes are tender.
Serves 6 to 8.

Cheesy Sausage-Potato Casserole

Buffalo Chicken Quinoa Casserole

Trish McGregor, Prospect, VA

1 c. quinoa, uncooked
3 c. shredded Cheddar
  cheese, divided
1 c. buffalo wing sauce,
  divided
1 c. sour cream
1/4 c. butter, softened

1/4 c. milk
1/2 t. garlic salt
1/4 t. pepper
1 t. dried basil
4 boneless, skinless
  chicken breasts, cooked
  and cubed

Cook quinoa according to package directions.
Meanwhile, in a large bowl, combine 2 cups cheese and
1/2 cup buffalo wing sauce with remaining ingredients
except chicken and quinoa. Fold in quinoa. Spread
mixture into a greased 13"x9" baking pan. Top with
chicken. Drizzle with remaining buffalo wing sauce
and sprinkle with remaining cheese. Bake, covered, at
350 degrees for 45 minutes, or until heated through and
bubbly. Serves 8.

Quick tip

Casseroles spell comfort food, but what
if the recipe is large and your family is small?
Simple...just divide the casserole ingredients
into two small dishes and freeze one
for later!

Buffalo Chicken Quinoa Casserole

Garlic Shrimp

Garlic Shrimp

Kathy Grashoff, Fort Wayne, IN

24 large shrimp, peeled
  and cleaned
1/4 c. olive oil
1/4 c. fresh parsley,
  chopped
3 cloves garlic, minced
1/2 t. red pepper flakes

1/4 t. pepper
1/4 c. butter, melted
1/2 c. seasoned dry bread
  crumbs
1/2 c. grated Parmesan
  cheese

Arrange shrimp in an ungreased 11"x7" baking pan; drizzle oil over shrimp. Combine the next 4 ingredients; sprinkle over shrimp. Cover and bake at 300 degrees for 15 minutes. Turn shrimp over. Drizzle with butter; sprinkle with bread crumbs and cheese. Bake, uncovered, for an additional 5 to 10 minutes. Serves 2.

Beefy Spinach Casserole

Bec Popovich, Columbus, OH

1 lb. ground beef
10-oz. pkg. frozen chopped
  spinach, thawed and
  drained
1 clove garlic, minced
salt and pepper to taste
16-oz. pkg. wide egg
  noodles, uncooked

10-3/4 oz. can cream of
  mushroom soup
2-1/2 c. milk
1 c. American cheese,
  shredded

Brown beef in a skillet over medium heat; drain. Add spinach, garlic, salt and pepper; cook until heated through. Stir in egg noodles; spoon into a greased 13"x9" baking pan and set aside. Combine soup and milk; mix well to blend and stir gently into beef mixture. Sprinkle with cheese. Bake at 325 degrees for 45 minutes, until bubbly. Serves 8.

Chicken Alfre

Jenny Unternahrer, W

6 c. penne pasta, u
3 boneless, skinles
  chicken breasts,
2 to 3 t. olive oil
2 zucchini, diced
2 yellow squash,
1 green or red pepper,
  diced

Cook pasta according to package directions; drain. Meanwhile, in a large skillet over medium heat, cook chicken in oil until nearly done. Add vegetables and cook almost to desired tenderness. In a large bowl, combine chicken mixture and pasta; stir in Alfredo sauce. Transfer to 2 greased 2-quart casserole dishes; top with cheese. Wrap and freeze one dish for later (thaw before baking). Bake, uncovered, at 350 degrees for 30 minutes, until bubbly and cheese is melted. Serves 4 to 6.

Delicious Dinners

Crab & Shri

Jennie Gist, Goos

2 8-oz. cans
  drained
2 4-oz.
  drai
2 c.

Quick tip

Store large bottles of olive oil in the refrigerator to keep it fresh. Pour a little into a small bottle to keep in the cupboard for everyday use.

...mp Casserole
...berry Patch

...rabmeat,

...ns tiny shrimp,
...ed

...elery, chopped

...green pepper, chopped

1 onion, chopped

1 T. Worcestershire sauce

1 t. sugar

1 c. mayonnaise

salt and pepper to taste

1 c. soft bread crumbs,
  buttered

2 T. lemon juice

Garnish: thin lemon slices

Mix together all ingredients except bread crumbs, lemon juice and garnish. Place in a greased 13"x9" baking pan. Spread bread crumbs over crab mixture. Bake, uncovered, at 350 degrees for 30 to 45 minutes, until heated through. Sprinkle lemon juice over casserole. Garnish with lemon slices. Serves 4 to 6.

Crab & Shrimp Casserole

Cheesy Zucchini & Beef Casserole
Lori Joy, Texico, IL

1 lb. ground beef

1 lb. ground pork sausage

2 c. zucchini, diced

1 c. onion, diced

1 c. green pepper, diced

1 c. tomato, diced

1 c. water

1/2 c. shell macaroni,
  uncooked

2 to 3 t. dried oregano

2 t. salt

2 c. shredded Cheddar
  cheese

2 c. shredded mozzarella
  cheese

Brown beef and sausage well in a skillet over medium heat; drain. Add vegetables, water, uncooked macaroni, oregano and salt. Bring to a boil, stirring often. Reduce heat to low. Simmer for 25 minutes, or until vegetables and macaroni are tender and liquid is almost absorbed. Stir occasionally, adding a little more water if too dry. Remove from heat; cover and let stand 10 to 15 minutes. Stir in Cheddar cheese. Spoon into a greased 13"x9" baking pan; sprinkle with mozzarella cheese. Bake, uncovered, at 375 degrees until golden and cheese is melted, 5 to 10 minutes. Makes 6 to 8 servings.

Baked Mostaccioli
Connie Bryant, Topeka, KS

1 lb. ground beef

8-oz. pkg. mostaccioli
  pasta, cooked

30-oz. jar spaghetti sauce

3/4 c. grated Parmesan
  cheese, divided

8-oz. pkg. shredded
  mozzarella cheese

Optional: additional grated
  Parmesan cheese

Brown ground beef in a large skillet; drain. Stir in cooked pasta, sauce and 1/2 cup Parmesan cheese; spoon into a greased 13"x9" baking pan. Top with mozzarella and remaining Parmesan cheese. Bake for 20 minutes at 375 degrees, until heated through. If desired, sprinkle with additional Parmesan cheese. Makes 6 servings.

Cheesy Zucchini & Beef Casserole

Blue-Ribbon Ham Casserole

Blue-Ribbon Ham Casserole

Laura Jones, Louisville, KY

1-1/2 lbs. yams, boiled,
  peeled and sliced
  3/4-inch thick
2 c. cooked ham, chopped
1-1/2 c. Golden Delicious
  apples, peeled, cored
  and sliced

1/4 t. salt
1/4 t. paprika
1/2 c. brown sugar, packed
2 T. bourbon or apple juice
2 T. butter

Arrange half the yams in a greased 2-quart round casserole dish; set aside. Layer ham evenly over yams, then layer apples evenly over ham. Arrange remaining yams over the apples; sprinkle with salt and paprika. Set aside. Combine brown sugar and bourbon or apple juice; sprinkle evenly over ingredients in dish. Dot with butter. Bake, covered, for 20 minutes. Baste with pan juices; bake, uncovered, for an additional 25 minutes. Baste and serve. Makes 6 servings.

Baked Chicken Jambalaya

Vicki Holland, Hampton, GA

1 lb. pkg. smoked beef
  sausage, sliced
1/4 c. butter
4 c. cooked chicken, cubed
16-oz. pkg. frozen mixed
  vegetables, thawed
1 onion, sliced

4 stalks celery, sliced
1 green pepper, thinly
  sliced
2 c. shredded mozzarella
  or Cheddar cheese
16-oz. pkg. bowtie pasta,
  cooked

In a skillet over medium-high heat, sauté sausage in butter until browned. Add chicken to skillet with sausage. Transfer sausage mixture into a 13"x9" baking pan; add mixed vegetables, onion, celery and green pepper. Top with cheese and cover with aluminum foil. Bake at 350 degrees for about 30 minutes, or until veggies are crisp-tender and cheese is melted. Serve over pasta. Serves 8.

Delicious Dinners

Pork Chops & B
Barbara Girlardo, Pittsb

6 pork chops
1 T. oil
10-3/4 oz. can
  chicken so
1 c. celery
1 c. oni

Bro
he

Baked Chicken Jambalaya

Quick tip

Chicken thighs may be used in most recipes calling for chicken breasts. They're juicier, more flavorful and budget-friendly too.

...iscuit Stuffing

...urgh, PA

1/4 t. pepper
1/8 t. poultry seasoning
1 egg, beaten
12-oz. tube refrigerated
  biscuits

...cream of
...p
..., diced
...n, diced

...wn pork chops in oil in a large skillet over medium ...at. Arrange chops in a greased 13"x9" baking pan; set ...side. Combine remaining ingredients except biscuits in a mixing bowl; set aside. Using a pizza cutter, cut each biscuit into 8 pieces. Fold into soup mixture and spoon over chops. Bake at 350 degrees for 45 to 55 minutes, until biscuits are golden. Makes 6 servings.

Ham & Cauliflower Casserole

Darrell Lawry, Kissimmee, FL

3 c. cooked ham, cubed
3 c. cauliflower flowerets,
  cooked
1-1/2 c. sliced mushrooms
salt and pepper to taste
2 T. butter

2 T. all-purpose flour
1 c. milk
1/2 c. sour cream
1 c. shredded Cheddar
  cheese
1 T. dry bread crumbs

Combine ham, cauliflower and mushrooms in an ungreased 3-quart casserole dish. Sprinkle with salt and pepper and set aside. Melt butter in a saucepan; stir in flour and milk. Cook over medium heat, stirring frequently, until thickened. Stir in sour cream and cheese; continue cooking until cheese has melted and sauce is smooth. Set aside; pour sauce over ham mixture. Sprinkle with bread crumbs. Bake at 350 degrees for 30 to 40 minutes, until heated through. Serves 6.

Cajun Seafood Fettucine

Sheila Collier, Kingwood, TX

1-1/2 c. butter, divided
2 8-oz. pkgs. frozen
  seasoned vegetable blend
garlic powder and Cajun
  seasoning to taste
1/4 c. all-purpose flour
1 pt. half-and-half
16-oz. pkg. pasteurized
  processed cheese spread,
  cubed

1-1/2 lbs. medium shrimp,
  peeled and cleaned
1-1/2 lbs. crabmeat
12-oz. pkg. egg noodles,
  cooked
12-oz. pkg. shredded
  Colby-Jack cheese

Melt 1-1/4 cups butter in a large saucepan; add vegetables and sauté until tender. Sprinkle with garlic powder and Cajun seasoning; set aside. Add enough water to flour to make a thick yet pourable paste; add to skillet. Stir in half-and-half and cheese spread; continue stirring until cheese is melted. Set aside. In a separate skillet, sauté shrimp in remaining butter until no longer pink. Add shrimp and crabmeat to vegetable mixture and let simmer on medium-low heat for 20 minutes. Stir in egg noodles; pour into an ungreased 13"x9" baking pan. Sprinkle with Colby-Jack cheese. Bake at 350 degrees for 20 minutes. Makes 8-10 servings.

Quick tip

Dress up tube biscuits by brushing the tops of each biscuit lightly with beaten egg and arranging a fresh parsley leaf on each. Lightly brush again with egg and bake as directed.

Cajun Seafood Fettucine

Delicious Dinners

Layered Southwestern Bake
Laura Fuller, Fort Wayne, IN

1 lb. ground beef
2 onions, chopped
1 green pepper, chopped
1/4 c. frozen green peas
1/2 t. chili powder
1/2 t. red pepper flakes
14-1/2 oz. can diced
  tomatoes, drained
1/4 c. tomato paste

15-1/4 oz. can kidney
  beans, drained and
  rinsed
11-oz. can corn, drained
4 6-inch corn tortillas,
  quartered
1/3 c. shredded Cheddar
  cheese

Combine beef, onions and pepper in a large skillet; cook over medium heat until beef is browned and onions are tender. Drain. Add peas; sprinkle with chili powder and red pepper flakes. Stir in tomatoes and tomato paste; reduce heat to low and simmer for 5 minutes. Add beans and corn; stir to combine. Spoon half the mixture into a greased 11"x7" baking pan; top with half the tortilla quarters. Layer with remaining beef mixture. Cover and bake at 350 degrees for 25 minutes; remove cover and top with remaining tortillas and cheese. Bake an additional 10 minutes, or until cheese is melted.

Quick tip

To spice up familiar casserole recipes, use various cheeses like smoked hot pepper or Pepper Jack. Cayenne pepper, chopped pickled jalapeños or fresh jalapeño peppers will also turn up the heat!

Layered Southwestern Bake

Cheesy Spinach & Sausage Bake

Cheesy Spinach & Sausage Bake

Rhonda Reeder, Ellicott City, MD

1 lb. ground Italian sausage
8-oz. can tomato sauce
10-oz. pkg. frozen chopped spinach, thawed and drained
2 c. cottage cheese
1/2 c. grated Parmesan cheese
1 egg, beaten
2 c. shredded mozzarella cheese

Brown sausage in a large skillet over medium heat; stir in tomato sauce and heat through. Set aside. Combine spinach, cottage cheese, Parmesan cheese and egg in a large bowl. Mix well and spread into a lightly greased 13"x9" baking pan. Spoon sausage mixture over spinach mixture and top with mozzarella cheese. Bake at 350 degrees for 40 minutes. Serves 8.

Oriental Beef & Rice

Tami Meyer, Plant City, FL

1 lb. ground beef
1 onion, chopped
salt and pepper to taste
1 c. instant rice, uncooked
10-3/4 oz. can cream of mushroom soup
10-3/4 oz. can cream of chicken soup
1 c. warm water
1/4 c. soy sauce

Combine beef, onion, salt and pepper in a skillet; cook over medium heat until beef is browned and onion is tender. Drain; set aside. Mix rice, soups, water and soy sauce together; stir in beef mixture. Spoon into a lightly greased 13"x9" baking pan; bake at 350 degrees for 50 minutes. Serves 4 to 6.

Pork Chop Potato Bake

Jackie Flood, Geneseo, NY

1 T. oil
6 boneless pork chops
seasoned salt and pepper
  to taste
1 c. shredded Cheddar
  cheese, divided
10-3/4 oz. can cream of
  mushroom soup

1/2 c. milk
1/2 c. sour cream
28-oz. pkg. frozen diced
  potatoes with onions and
  peppers, thawed
1 to 2 T. onion soup mix

Heat oil in a skillet over medium-high heat. Season pork chops with salt and pepper; brown in oil for 5 minutes per side, until golden. In a bowl, combine 1/2 cup cheese and remaining ingredients. Spread cheese mixture in a greased 3-quart casserole dish. Arrange pork chops over top. Bake, covered, at 350 degrees for 40 minutes. Top with remaining cheese. Bake, uncovered, for an additional 10 minutes, or until cheese is melted. Serves 6.

Pork Chop Potato Bake

Kohlrabi Gratin

Katja Meyer-Thuerke, Wattenbek, Germany

1-1/2 lbs. kohlrabi, peeled
  and thinly sliced
1/4 c. oil, divided
2-1/4 c. cooked turkey
  breast, thinly sliced
salt, pepper and nutmeg to
  taste
2 onions, diced

1 c. whipping cream
1 c. cream cheese with
  herbs
1/2 c. fresh chives, finely
  chopped
1/2 c. Gruyère cheese,
  grated

Cook kohlrabi in boiling salted water for 2 to 3 minutes. Rinse with cold water; drain. Heat 2 tablespoons oil in a saucepan over medium-high heat. Cook turkey until golden; add seasonings to taste. Remove from pan and set aside. To the same skillet, add remaining oil and onions. Sauté until golden. Stir in cream and cream cheese. Season again to taste. Reduce heat to medium; stir in chives. Butter a 11"x7" baking pan and layer alternately kohlrabi and turkey in pan. Pour cream sauce over top; sprinkle with Gruyère cheese. Bake, uncovered, at 350 degrees for about 20 minutes. Serves 4.

Kohlrabi Gratin

Creamy Ham & Biscuits

Apple-Pork Chop Casserole

Gayla Reyes, Hamilton, OH

1 T. oil
8 boneless pork chops
2 6-oz. pkgs. herb-flavored
  stuffing mix
2 21-oz. cans apple pie
  filling

Heat oil in a skillet over medium-high heat. Cook pork chops in oil until both sides are browned. Meanwhile, prepare stuffing according to package directions. Pour pie filling into a lightly greased 13"x9" baking pan; lay pork chops on top. Cover with stuffing. Bake, uncovered, at 325 degrees for 45 minutes to one hour, until pork chops are cooked through. Serves 8.

Creamy Ham & Biscuits

Maggie Antonelli, Vancouver, WA

1/2 c. butter, sliced
1-1/2 c. frozen peas &
  carrots
4-oz. can sliced
  mushrooms, drained and
  liquid reserved
1/2 c. all-purpose flour
1 t. salt
1/2 t. pepper
1 t. garlic powder
1-1/2 c. milk
1-1/4 c. very hot water
3/4 lb. cooked ham, diced
4-oz. jar diced pimentos,
  drained
16-oz. tube refrigerated
  jumbo buttermilk
  biscuits

Melt butter in a large skillet over medium heat. Add peas & carrots and mushrooms; cook for 5 minutes. Add flour and seasonings; stir continually until bubbly. Remove skillet from heat. Stirring well, gradually add milk, then reserved mushroom liquid, then hot water. Return skillet to medium heat. Bring mixture to a boil; continue to boil and stir for one minute. Stir in ham and pimentos. Spoon mixture into a greased 13"x9" baking pan; arrange unbaked biscuits on top. Bake, uncovered, at 375 degrees for 15 minutes, or until bubbly and biscuits are golden. Makes 8 servings.

Apple-Pork Chop Casserole

Veggie Hodge-Podge

Shelley Wallace, Troy, IL

1 to 2 T. olive oil
2 to 3 boneless, skinless
  chicken breasts, cooked
  and cubed
1 to 2 andouille or
  Kielbasa sausage, sliced
1 to 2 sweet potatoes,
  peeled and cubed
1 bunch broccoli, cut into
  flowerets
1/2 head cauliflower, cut
  into flowerets
1 lb. green beans, cut up
1 zucchini, sliced
1 yellow squash, sliced
1 onion, sliced
4 t. garlic, minced
salt and pepper to taste

Spread oil in the bottom of a 13"x9" baking pan; set aside. In a large bowl, combine remaining ingredients. Toss to mix well. Transfer to pan; cover with aluminum foil. Bake at 350 degrees for one to 1-1/2 hours, until vegetables are tender. Makes about 8 servings.

Meat & Potato Pie

Meat & Potato Pie

Punki Gehring, Allyn, WA

1/2 lb. ground beef
1/2 lb. ground turkey
1/2 onion, chopped
14-oz. can sauerkraut, drained
4 c. instant mashed potatoes, cooked
2 c. shredded Swiss cheese

Brown beef, turkey and onion together in a large skillet over medium heat. Place mixture into an ungreased 13"x9" baking pan. Cover beef mixture with sauerkraut; top with mashed potatoes. Bake at 350 degrees for 30 to 35 minutes, or until potatoes are golden. Top with cheese and bake an additional 5 minutes, or until cheese is melted. Makes 4 to 6 servings.

Parmesan Potatoes & Ham

Stephanie Mayer, Portsmouth, VA

10-3/4 oz. can cream of celery soup
1/2 c. milk
pepper to taste
2 potatoes, peeled and sliced
1 onion, sliced
2 c. cooked ham, diced
2 T. grated Parmesan cheese

Combine soup, milk and pepper in an ungreased 8"x8" baking pan. Layer potatoes, onion and ham over top. Bake, covered, at 375 degrees for one hour. Sprinkle with cheese and bake, uncovered for an additional 20 minutes. Serves 6.

Quick tip

Start dinner with a cup of hot soup to take the edge off appetites...it's a super meal stretcher!

Hamburger Noodle Casserole

Hamburger Noodle Casserole

Gloria Kirkland, Pearson, GA

16-oz. pkg. wide egg noodles, uncooked
1-3/4 lbs. lean ground beef
1 onion, chopped
1 green pepper, chopped
1 t. salt
1 t. pepper
26-oz. can cream of mushroom soup
12-oz. pkg. shredded Cheddar cheese

Cook noodles according to package directions. Drain; set aside. Meanwhile, in a skillet over medium heat, brown beef with onion, green pepper, salt and pepper; drain. Combine beef mixture, noodles and soup. Pour into a greased 13"x9" baking pan; top with cheese. Bake, uncovered, at 325 degrees for 10 to 15 minutes, until cheese is melted and bubbly. Serves 6 to 8.

Taco-Filled Pasta Shells

Brittany Cornelius, Chambersburg, PA

2 lbs. ground beef
2 1-1/4 oz. pkgs. taco
  seasoning mix
8-oz. pkg. cream cheese,
  cubed
2 12-oz. pkgs. jumbo pasta
  shells, uncooked
1/4 c. butter, melted
1 c. salsa

1 c. taco sauce
1 c. shredded Cheddar
  cheese
1 c. shredded Monterey
  Jack cheese
1-1/2 c. tortilla chips,
  crushed
Optional: sour cream,
  chopped green onions

Brown beef in a skillet over medium heat; drain. Add taco seasoning and cook according to package directions. Add cream cheese; stir to melt. Remove beef mixture to a bowl and chill for one hour. Meanwhile, cook pasta shells according to package directions; drain. Toss shells with butter. Fill each shell with 3 tablespoons of beef mixture. Spoon salsa into a greased 13"x9" baking pan; place shells on top of salsa and cover with taco sauce. Bake, covered, at 350 degrees for 30 minutes. Uncover, sprinkle with cheeses and tortilla chips. Bake for 15 minutes, or until heated through. Serves 8.

Southwestern Turkey Casserole

Amy Butcher, Columbus, GA

10-3/4 oz. can cream of
  chicken soup
10-3/4 oz. can cream of
  mushroom soup
7-oz. can diced green
  chiles, drained
1 c. sour cream

16 6-inch corn tortillas,
  cut into strips
2 c. cooked turkey, diced
  and divided
8-oz. pkg. shredded
  Cheddar cheese, divided

Combine soups, chiles and sour cream in a mixing bowl; set aside. Line the bottom of a 13"x9" baking pan with half the tortilla strips. Top with half the turkey. Spread half the soup mixture over turkey; sprinkle with half the cheese. Repeat layers. Bake at 350 degrees for 30 to 45 minutes. Makes 6 to 8 servings.

Quick tip

Stir up some simple artichoke salsa to spoon over casserole dishes! Drain and finely chop one, 6-ounce jar of marinated artichoke hearts and blend with one finely chopped chile pepper, one minced garlic clove and the juice of one lime.

Taco-Filled Pasta Shells

Not-So-Stuffed Cabbage

Not-So-Stuffed Cabbage

Michelle Bogie, Clio, MI

8-oz. can tomato sauce

10-3/4 oz. can tomato soup

1 T. brown sugar, packed

1/2 c. chicken broth or water

1 lb. ground beef, turkey or pork

1 onion, chopped

1 to 2 T. Worcestershire sauce

garlic powder, seasoning salt and pepper to taste

1 head cabbage, chopped and divided

4 potatoes, peeled and cubed

Optional: 1 c. mild salsa

In a bowl, stir together sauce, soup, brown sugar and chicken broth or water; set aside. In a separate large bowl, combine meat, onion, Worcestershire sauce and seasonings; mix gently and set aside. In a greased 3-quart casserole dish, layer half each of cabbage and potatoes; crumble in half of meat mixture. Pour half of sauce mixture over the top. Repeat, ending with sauce mixture. If desired, pour salsa over the top. Cover and bake at 350 degrees for one hour. Uncover; bake for an additional 30 minutes. Makes 6 servings.

Hobo Dinner

Denise Piccirilli, Huber Heights, OH

1-1/2 lbs. ground beef

1 t. Worcestershire sauce

1/2 t. seasoned pepper

1/8 t. garlic powder

3 redskin potatoes, sliced

1 onion, sliced

3 carrots, peeled and sliced

olive oil and dried parsley to taste

In a bowl, combine beef, Worcestershire sauce, pepper and garlic powder; form into 4 to 6 patties. Place each patty on an 18-inch length of aluminum foil. Divide slices of potato, onion and carrots evenly and place on top of each patty. Sprinkle with olive oil and parsley to taste. Wrap tightly in aluminum foil and arrange packets on a baking sheet. Bake at 375 degrees for one hour, or until vegetables are tender and beef is cooked through. Serves 4 to 6.

Hobo Dinner

Salisbury Steak with Potatoes

Alisha Walker, Eagar, AZ

4 potatoes, peeled and sliced

1-1/2 lbs. ground beef

1 c. soft bread crumbs

1 egg, beaten

1 onion, chopped

26-oz. can cream of mushroom soup

1-1/2 oz. pkg. beefy onion soup mix

Arrange potatoes in a lightly greased 13"x9" baking pan. Combine ground beef, bread crumbs, egg and onion; form into 6 patties. Place patties on top of potato slices. Combine soup and dry soup mix; blend well. Pour over patties and potatoes. Bake at 350 degrees for 1-1/2 hours. Serves 6.

Beef & Potato Casserole

Robin Hill, Rochester, NY

2 T. shortening
2 lbs. stew beef, cubed
1 onion, thinly sliced
1 c. water
10-3/4 oz. can cream of mushroom soup
1 c. sour cream
1-1/4 c. milk
1 t. salt
1/4 t. pepper
4 potatoes, peeled and diced
1 c. shredded Cheddar cheese
1-1/4 c. whole-grain wheat flake cereal, crushed

Melt shortening in a large skillet over high heat. Add beef and onion; cook until browned. Drain; stir in water and bring to a boil. Cover; reduce heat to low and simmer for 30 minutes. Set aside. Combine soup, sour cream, milk, salt and pepper in a medium bowl; mix well. Pour beef mixture into an ungreased 13"x9" baking pan; arrange potatoes over beef. Pour soup mixture over potatoes; sprinkle with cheese and cereal. Bake, uncovered, at 350 degrees for 1-1/2 hours. Serves 6 to 8.

Quick tip

Perfect pasta! Fill a large pot with water and bring to a rolling boil. Add a tablespoon of salt. Stir in pasta. Boil, uncovered, for the time suggested on package. There's no need to add oil...frequent stirring will keep pasta from sticking together.

Super-Simple Baked Peppers

Crystal Branstrom, Russell, PA

3 green peppers, quartered
1 lb. ground beef
1/2 lb. ground Italian pork sausage
2 onions, chopped
garlic powder to taste
salt and pepper to taste
26-oz. jar spaghetti sauce
2 c. long-cooking rice, cooked
16-oz. pkg. pasteurized process cheese spread, sliced

Arrange peppers in a lightly greased 13"x9" baking pan; set aside. In a large skillet over medium heat, brown ground beef, sausage and onions with garlic powder, salt and pepper; drain. Stir in sauce and rice. Pour over peppers; top with sliced cheese. Cover with aluminum foil. Bake at 350 degrees for one hour. Serves 6 to 8.

Sour Cream Noodle Bake

Sandy Coffey, Cincinnati, OH

8-oz. pkg. wide egg noodles, uncooked
1 lb. ground beef
8-oz. can tomato sauce
1/4 t. garlic powder
1 t. salt
1/8 t. pepper
1 c. cottage cheese
1 c. sour cream
1 T. butter, melted
6 green onions, chopped
3/4 c. shredded Cheddar cheese

Cook noodles according to package directions; drain. Meanwhile, in a skillet over medium heat, brown beef; drain. Stir tomato sauce, garlic powder, salt and pepper into beef; simmer for 5 minutes. Add cottage cheese, sour cream, butter and onions to noodles; mix gently. In a greased 2-quart casserole dish, alternate layers of noodle mixture and beef mixture; top with shredded cheese. Bake, uncovered, at 350 degrees for 20 minutes, or until cheese is melted and golden. Makes 6 to 8 servings.

Super-Simple Baked Peppers

Taco Hot Bake

Taco Hot Bake

KellyJean Gettelfinger, Sellersburg, IN

2 lbs. ground beef
2 1-1/4 oz. pkgs. taco
  seasoning mix
1-1/3 c. water
6-oz. pkg. chili cheese corn
  chips
2 10-3/4 oz. cans Cheddar
  cheese soup
1 c. milk
16-oz. pkg. shredded
  mozzarella cheese,
  divided
Garnish: sour cream,
  shredded lettuce, halved
  cherry tomatoes, sliced
  black olives, sliced
  mushrooms

Brown beef in a large skillet over medium heat; drain.
Stir in taco seasoning and water; bring to a boil. Reduce
heat to low; simmer for 5 minutes, stirring occasionally.
Spread corn chips evenly in a lightly greased 13"x9"
baking pan. Spoon beef mixture over chips; set aside.
In a saucepan over medium-low heat, stir soup and milk
until smooth and heated through. Spoon soup mixture
over beef mixture. Top with 3 cups cheese. Bake,
uncovered, at 350 degrees for 10 to 15 minutes, until
hot and bubbly. Remove from oven; top with remaining
cheese. Garnish individual portions with desired
toppings. Serves 6 to 8.

Warm & Wonderful Chicken Salad

Warm & Wonderful Chicken Salad

Susan Fracker, New Concord, OH

2 c. cooked chicken,
  shredded
2 c. celery, diced
1 T. onion, grated
1 c. mayonnaise
1/2 c. slivered almonds
1/2 t. lemon juice
1-1/2 c. shredded Cheddar
  cheese, divided
1/2 c. potato chips, crushed

Mix chicken, celery, onion, mayonnaise, almonds, lemon
juice and one cup cheese in a greased 13"x9" baking pan.
Top with remaining cheese and chips. Bake, uncovered,
at 450 degrees for 15 to 20 minutes, until hot and bubbly.
Serves 6 to 8.

Chicken Bombay

MaryBeth Summers, Medford, OR

1/4 c. butter, melted
1 T. curry powder
1 tart apple, peeled, cored
  and chopped
1 onion, chopped
3 lbs. chicken, cut up
2 c. cooked rice

Spread butter in a 13"x9" baking pan; add curry powder
and mix well. Stir in apple and onion. Bake, uncovered,
at 400 degrees for 5 minutes. Add chicken to pan, skin-
side down. Cover and bake for 25 minutes. Turn chicken
over and bake, uncovered, an additional 25 minutes,
or until chicken juices run clear. Remove chicken to
a serving platter; stir cooked rice into pan juices and
serve. Makes 4 servings.

Delicious Dinners

Green Bean, Ham & Potato Bake
Rachel Kowasic, Connellsville, PA

1 onion, chopped
2 cloves garlic, minced
1 T. butter
3 potatoes, diced
salt and pepper to taste
2 14-1/2 oz. cans green
   beans, drained
1-1/2 c. cooked ham, cubed
2 sprigs fresh rosemary,
   chopped
1 c. water

In a skillet over medium-high heat, sauté onion and garlic in butter; add potatoes, salt and pepper. Cook until potatoes are crisp. In a greased 13"x9" baking pan, combine potato mixture, green beans, ham and rosemary. Drizzle water over all. Cover with aluminum foil and bake at 350 degrees for one hour, or until potatoes are tender. Serves 6.

Green Bean, Ham & Potato Bake

Pork Chop Au Gratin
Linda Karner, Pisgah Forest, NC

6 to 8 pork chops
1 t. salt
1 to 2 T. oil
2 c. water
2 carrots, peeled and
   thinly sliced
10-oz. pkg. frozen Italian
   green beans
2 T. butter
7-oz. pkg. au gratin potato
   mix
10-3/4 oz. can cream of
   celery soup
2/3 c. milk
2 T. Dijon mustard
1/2 t. dried basil
1/2 t. Worcestershire sauce

Sprinkle pork chops with salt. Brown in oil in a skillet over medium heat; set aside. Heat water to boiling in a saucepan; add carrots and beans. Return to a boil; stir in butter, potato slices and sauce from mix. Remove from heat and set aside. Mix soup, milk, mustard, basil and Worcestershire sauce; stir into vegetable mixture and pour into an ungreased 13"x9" baking pan. Arrange chops on top. Cover and bake at 350 degrees for 45 minutes; uncover and bake an additional 15 minutes, until chops are tender. Let stand 5 minutes before serving. Makes 6 to 8 servings.

Pork Chop Au Gratin

Tangy Citrus Chicken

Tangy Citrus Chicken
Jo Ann

8 boneless, skinless
  chicken breasts
6-oz. can frozen lemonade,
  thawed
3/4 c. molasses

1 t. dried savory
1/2 t. ground mustard
1/2 t. dried thyme
1/2 t. lemon juice

Place chicken in a 13"x9" baking pan coated with
non-stick vegetable spray. In a medium mixing bowl,
combine remaining ingredients; mix well. Pour half of
the mixture over the chicken. Bake, uncovered, at
350 degrees for 20 minutes. Turn chicken; add
remaining sauce. Bake an additional 15 to 20 minutes,
or until juices run clear. Makes 8 servings.

Ham-It-Up Casserole
Lisa Bownas, Columbus, OH

16-oz. pkg. frozen French
  fries
16-oz. pkg. frozen chopped
  broccoli, cooked
1-1/2 c. cooked ham, cubed
10-3/4 oz. can cream of
  mushroom soup

1-1/4 c. milk
1/4 c. mayonnaise
1 c. grated Parmesan
  cheese

Arrange fries in a greased 13"x9" baking pan. Top with
broccoli; sprinkle with ham and set aside. Combine soup,
milk and mayonnaise in a small bowl; mix well and pour
evenly over ham. Sprinkle with cheese. Bake, uncovered,
at 375 degrees for 40 minutes. Serves 4 to 6.

Oven Beef & Noodles
Kristie Rigo, Friedens, PA

1-1/2 oz. pkg. onion soup
  mix
4 c. water
10-3/4 oz. can cream of
  mushroom soup

3-lb. boneless beef chuck
  roast
12-oz. pkg. kluski egg
  noodles, uncooked

Combine soup mix and water in a roasting pan; stir in
soup. Place roast in pan on top of soup mixture. Cover
and bake at 350 degrees for 4 hours, or until roast is
very tender. Remove roast from pan and shred; return
to pan. Add noodles to pan; reduce heat to 300 degrees.
Cover and bake for 20 to 30 minutes, stirring every
15 minutes until noodles are tender. Add water if
necessary to prevent drying out. Makes 6 to 8 servings.

Oven Beef & Noodles

Baked Pork Chop Suey

Evelyn Hammen, Little Chute, WI

2 T. oil
5 T. soy sauce
2 lbs. boneless pork steaks,
  cut into bite-size cubes
4-oz. can sliced
  mushrooms
10-3/4 oz. can cream of
  mushroom soup
10-3/4 oz. can chicken &
  rice soup
8-oz. can sliced water
  chestnuts, drained
14-oz. can bean sprouts,
  drained

2 c. celery, diced
1 onion, chopped
2-2/3 c. water
1 T. browning and
  seasoning sauce
1 t. salt
1/2 t. pepper
cooked rice
Garnish: steamed chow
  mein noodles

Heat oil and soy sauce in a deep skillet over medium heat. Brown pork on all sides. Transfer pork mixture to an ungreased 13"x9" baking pan. Add undrained mushrooms and remaining ingredients except rice and garnish; mix well. Bake, covered, at 350 degrees for 1-1/2 hours. Serve over cooked rice, topped with steamed chow mein noodles. Serves 8.

Mile-High Pork Chop Casserole

Karen Shepherd, Elko, NV

4 pork chops
salt and pepper to taste
2 T. oil
1 c. long-cooking rice,
  uncooked

1 tomato, sliced
1 green pepper, sliced
1 onion, sliced
10-oz. can beef consommé

Sprinkle pork chops on both sides with salt and pepper. Heat oil in a skillet; cook chops on both sides until golden. Set aside. Sprinkle rice in a lightly greased 11"x7" baking pan. Arrange pork chops on top of rice. Place tomato, green pepper and onion slices on top of each pork chop. Pour consommé over all; cover. Bake at 350 degrees for 1-1/2 hours, or until pork chops are tender and rice has absorbed all the liquid. Makes 4 servings.

Quick tip

Don't pass up a good deal on overripe produce! Past-their-prime zucchini, yellow squash, mushrooms, eggplant and sweet potatoes are delicious sliced and added to any casserole.

Baked Pork Chop Suey

Southern-Style Shrimp & Rice

Southern-Style Shrimp & Rice
Claire Bertram, Lexington, KY

3/4 c. butter, divided
1 onion, sliced
8-oz. pkg. sliced
  mushrooms
1/4 c. green pepper, diced
2 c. cooked long-grain and
  wild rice
1-1/2 lbs. medium shrimp,
  peeled and cleaned

1 T. Worcestershire sauce
hot pepper sauce to taste
salt and pepper to taste
1/2 c. all-purpose flour
1-1/2 c. chicken broth
1/2 c. white wine or
  chicken broth

In a large heavy skillet, melt 1/4 cup butter over medium heat. Add onion, mushrooms and pepper; sauté for 8 minutes. Add rice; toss until well blended and spread across bottom of a greased 2-quart casserole dish. Set aside. In a medium mixing bowl, combine shrimp, sauces, salt and pepper. Arrange evenly over vegetable mixture; set aside. Melt remaining butter over medium heat in a saucepan; add flour and whisk for one minute. Add broth and wine or additional broth. Whisk until well blended and slightly thickened; pour evenly over shrimp. Bake at 350 degrees for 25 minutes, until bubbly. Serves 6.

Quick tip

Here's a little trick to clean baked-on food from a casserole dish. Place a dryer sheet inside and fill with water. Let the dish sit overnight, then sponge clean. You'll find the fabric softeners will really soften the baked-on food.

Curry Chicken Casserole

Curry Chicken Casserole
Jodi Griggs, Richmond, KY

1 c. long-cooking rice,
  uncooked
14-1/2 oz. can French-cut
  green beans, drained and
  divided
3 c. cooked chicken,
  chopped
8-oz. can sliced water
  chestnuts, drained

10-3/4 oz. can cream of
  chicken soup
1/4 c. chicken broth
1 c. mayonnaise
1 t. curry powder
1 c. French fried onions

Cook rice according to package directions. Combine rice, half the beans and remaining ingredients except onions in a greased 3-quart baking pan; mix well. Top with remaining beans. Bake, uncovered, at 350 degrees for 25 minutes, or until bubbling. Sprinkle onions over top and bake for another 5 minutes. Serves 6.

Delicious Dinners

Gram's Upper-Crust Chicken

Sandy Coffey, Cincinnati, OH

8 slices bread	2 eggs, beaten
2 c. cooked chicken, cubed	1 c. mayonnaise
1 c. celery, chopped	1/2 t. salt
2 c. shredded Cheddar cheese, divided	1/2 t. poultry seasoning
	2 c. milk

Trim crusts from bread. Cut crusts into small cubes; set aside bread slices. In a bowl, mix crust cubes, chicken, celery and 1-3/4 cups cheese. Spoon into a greased 2-quart casserole dish. Cut bread slices into quarters and arrange on top of chicken mixture; set aside. In a separate bowl, whisk together eggs, mayonnaise and seasonings. Gradually add milk, mixing well. Spoon over chicken mixture. Sprinkle remaining cheese on top. Cover and refrigerate for 2 to 4 hours. Uncover; bake at 375 degrees for 30 to 40 minutes, until puffed and golden. Makes 4 servings.

Beef de Roma

Diane Hime, Corinth, NY

1 lb. ground beef	1/2 t. dried basil
1/2 c. onion, chopped	1/4 t. pepper
1/4 c. green pepper, chopped	2 8-oz. cans tomato sauce
1 clove garlic, minced	3 c. prepared rice
1 t. salt	16-oz. container cottage cheese
1 t. dried parsley	Garnish: grated Parmesan cheese
1/2 t. dried oregano	

Brown beef in a skillet; drain. Add onion, pepper, garlic, seasonings and tomato sauce; simmer 5 minutes. Layer rice, cottage cheese and beef mixture in a greased 3-quart casserole dish. Bake at 350 degrees for 30 minutes. Sprinkle with Parmesan cheese and bake 10 minutes, or until golden. Serves 4 to 6.

Family Favorite Beef & Noodles

Michele Nylander, Redding, CA

2 lbs. ground beef	8-oz. container sour cream
1 T. margarine	3/4 c. green onion, sliced
15-oz. can tomato sauce	3 c. fettuccine pasta, uncooked
2 cloves garlic, minced	1 c. shredded Cheddar cheese
1 t. sugar	Garnish: paprika
1 t. salt	
1 t. pepper	
8-oz. pkg. cream cheese, softened	

Brown ground beef in margarine in a skillet; drain. Add tomato sauce, garlic, sugar, salt and pepper; reduce heat and simmer for 20 minutes. In a medium bowl, beat cream cheese with a fork until fluffy; stir in sour cream and onion. Set aside. Cook fettuccine according to package instructions. Layer ingredients as follows in a greased 13"x9" baking pan: beef mixture, cooked fettuccine, cream cheese mixture, Cheddar cheese. Sprinkle with paprika; bake at 350 degrees for 25 to 30 minutes, or until bubbly. Serves 6 to 8.

Quick tip

Post a dinner wish list on the fridge and invite everyone to jot down their favorite dishes. Family members who are involved in meal planning are much more likely to look forward to family dinnertime together!

Gram's Upper-Crust Chicken

Sweet Pepper-Sausage Bake

Sweet Pepper-Sausage Bake

Lis McDonnell, New Castle, IN

3 T. olive oil, divided

14-oz. pkg. smoked pork sausage, sliced

3 to 4 potatoes, peeled and cubed

16-oz. pkg. mini sweet peppers, sliced

1 onion, sliced

salt and pepper to taste

Line a 13"x9" baking pan with aluminum foil. Brush one tablespoon oil over foil; set aside. Combine sausage and vegetables in a large bowl. Drizzle with remaining oil; mix to coat well and spread in pan. Season with salt and pepper. Cover with another layer of foil, sealing top and bottom of foil together. Bake at 350 degrees for 30 minutes, or until vegetables are tender. Serves 3 to 4.

Chicken & Asparagus Bake

Marilyn Morel, Keene, NH

6 boneless, skinless chicken breasts, cooked and cubed

3 14-1/2 oz. cans asparagus pieces, drained

2-oz. jar chopped pimentos, drained

3/4 c. slivered almonds

3 10-3/4 oz. cans cream of mushroom soup

2 2.8-oz. cans French fried onions

Layer chicken, asparagus, pimentos, almonds and soup in a lightly greased 2-1/2 quart casserole dish. Cover with aluminum foil; bake at 350 degrees for 30 to 40 minutes, until bubbly. Uncover and top with onions. Bake for an additional 5 minutes. Serves 6 to 8.

No-Peek Chicken & Rice

Jennie Gist, Gooseberry Patch

10-3/4 oz. can cream of mushroom soup

10-3/4 oz. can cream of celery soup

6-oz. pkg. long grain & wild rice mix, uncooked

1-1/4 c. water

1 t. dried parsley

1/8 t. curry powder

4 chicken breasts, or 8 chicken thighs and drumsticks

1.35-oz. pkg. onion soup mix

In a large bowl, mix soups, rice mix, seasoning packet from rice, water, parsley and curry powder. Spoon into a lightly greased 13"x9" baking pan. Remove skin from chicken, if desired. Arrange chicken on top of rice mixture; sprinkle soup mix over chicken. Cover tightly with aluminum foil. Bake at 350 degrees for 2-1/2 hours, or until rice is tender and chicken juices run clear when pierced. Serves 4.

Chicken & Asparagus Bake

Creamy Seafood Enchiladas

Kristie Rigo, Friedens, PA

12-oz. pkg. imitation
  crabmeat, flaked
10 10-inch flour tortillas
3 T. butter
1 onion, minced
2 cloves garlic, minced
1 t. coriander
1/2 t. salt
1/2 t. pepper

8-oz. container sour cream
3 T. all-purpose flour
14-1/2 oz. can chicken
  broth
2 4-oz. cans diced green
  chiles
1-1/2 c. shredded Monterey
  Jack cheese, divided

Place crabmeat in a medium bowl; set aside. Wrap tortillas in aluminum foil; bake at 350 degrees for 10 minutes, until softened. Set aside. Heat butter in a medium saucepan; add onion, garlic, coriander, salt and pepper. Cook until onion is transparent. Set aside. Combine sour cream and flour in a medium bowl; stir in broth. Add sour cream mixture and chiles to onion mixture in saucepan; cook over medium heat until thick and bubbly. Remove from heat; add 1/2 cup cheese. Add one cup of hot mixture to crabmeat; divide among softened tortillas, placing filling in middle of each tortilla. Roll up tortillas; arrange seam-side down in a greased 13"x9" baking pan and top with remaining sour cream mixture. Bake, covered, at 350 degrees for 30 to 35 minutes, until heated through. Sprinkle with remaining cheese. Bake, uncovered, for 5 additional minutes, until cheese is melted. Let stand 5 minutes before serving. Makes 4 to 6 servings.

Quick tip

If there's leftover salad after dinner, use it for a tasty sandwich filling the next day. Split a pita pocket, stuff with salad, chopped chicken or turkey, sliced grapes and drizzle with salad dressing.

Pantry Casserole

Vickie

1 lb. ground beef
2 t. poultry seasoning
2 t. dried thyme
1-1/2 t. ground cumin
salt and pepper to taste
2 t. garlic, minced
3 potatoes, thinly sliced
2 T. butter
1 onion, thinly sliced in
  rings

2 c. sliced mushrooms
10-3/4 oz. can cream of
  chicken soup
3/4 c. water
20 saltine crackers,
  crushed
Garnish: 1/8 t. paprika

Place ground beef in a large skillet; sprinkle with seasonings and garlic. Cook, stirring frequently, over medium heat until browned. Drain; transfer to an ungreased 13"x9" baking pan. Arrange 2 layers of sliced potatoes over beef mixture, sprinkling each layer with salt and pepper; set aside. Melt butter in the skillet over medium heat; sauté onion and mushrooms until crisp-tender. Spread over potatoes; set aside. Combine soup and water; spread evenly over casserole. Top with cracker crumbs and sprinkle with paprika. Cover with aluminum foil and bake for one hour, or until potatoes are soft. Remove foil and bake an additional 10 minutes, until golden. Serves 4 to 6

Crunchy Almond & Sausage Bake

Athena Colegrove, Big Springs, TX

1 lb. sausage link, sliced
1/4 c. onion, sliced
1 stalk celery, chopped
1 green pepper, chopped
1/2 c. long-grain rice,
  uncooked

4-1/2 oz. pkg. chicken
  noodle soup mix
2 c. hot water
1/2 c. slivered almonds

Combine sausage, onion, celery and green pepper in a large skillet over medium-high heat. Sauté for 5 minutes; drain. Stir in rice, soup mix and water. Transfer to a lightly greased 2-quart casserole dish; sprinkle with almonds. Bake, covered, at 300 degrees for 1-1/2 hours. Serves 4.

Creamy Seafood Enchiladas

Oodles of Noodles Chili Bake

Italian Lasagna

John Alexander, New Britain, CT

1 lb. ground Italian
   sausage
1 clove garlic, minced
1 T. fresh basil
1 T. dried oregano
2 t. salt, divided
32-oz. can whole tomatoes,
   chopped
2 6-oz. cans tomato paste

2 eggs, beaten
3 c. cottage cheese
1/2 c. grated Parmesan
   cheese
1/2 t. pepper
10-oz. pkg. lasagna, cooked
16-oz. pkg. shredded
   mozzarella cheese,
   divided

Brown Italian sausage in a large saucepan; drain. Add garlic, basil, oregano, 1-1/2 teaspoons salt and tomatoes. Simmer, uncovered, 30 minutes, stirring occasionally. Set aside. Blend together eggs, cottage cheese, Parmesan cheese, remaining salt and pepper. Set aside. Layer half the prepared lasagna in a lightly greased 13"x9" baking pan; spread with half the cottage cheese mixture. Add half the mozzarella and half the meat sauce. Repeat layering. Bake at 350 degrees for 45 minutes. Let stand 15 minutes before serving. Serves 8.

Oodles of Noodles Chili Bake

Robin Kessler, Fresno, CA

12-oz. pkg. wide egg
   noodles, uncooked
1 lb. ground beef
14-1/2 oz. can diced
   tomatoes

15-oz. can corn, drained
15-oz. can chili
1 c. shredded Cheddar
   cheese, divided

Cook noodles according to package directions; drain and set aside. Meanwhile, brown beef in a skillet over medium heat; drain. Combine tomatoes with juice and remaining ingredients except 1/4 cup cheese in a lightly greased 13"x9" baking pan. Top with remaining cheese. Bake, uncovered, at 350 degrees for about 20 minutes, or until heated through. Serves 4.

Julie's Chicken Pie

Julie's Chicken Pie

Julie Zahn, Syracuse, NE

4 c. cooked chicken, cubed
10-3/4 oz. can cream of
   chicken soup
10-1/2 oz. can chicken
   broth
1/2 t. poultry seasoning

16-oz. can sliced carrots,
   drained
1-1/2 c. all-purpose flour
2 t. baking powder
1-1/2 c. buttermilk
1/2 c. butter, melted

Place chicken in a lightly greased 3-quart casserole dish. Combine soup, broth and seasoning in a bowl; spoon over chicken. Arrange carrots on top. In another bowl, mix together flour and baking powder; stir in buttermilk and melted butter. Spoon over carrots. Bake, uncovered, at 350 degrees for one hour, or until bubbly and crust is golden. Serves 6.

Easy Weeknight Favorite

Sherry Gordon, Arlington Heights, IL

1-1/2 lbs. ground beef
14-1/2 oz. can diced
  tomatoes
1 t. salt
1 T. sugar
1-1/2 c. sour cream
3-oz. pkg. cream cheese,
  softened
1/4 c. onion, chopped
8-oz. pkg. medium egg
  noodles, cooked
1 c. shredded Cheddar
  cheese

Brown beef in a large skillet over medium heat; drain. Add tomatoes, salt and sugar; reduce to low heat and simmer for 15 minutes. Set aside. Combine sour cream, cream cheese and onion in a bowl; mix well and set aside. Place half the noodles in a lightly greased 13"x9" baking pan; top with beef mixture, then sour cream mixture. Layer remaining noodles over top; sprinkle with cheese. Bake at 350 degrees for 25 minutes. Serves 6.

Homestyle Turkey & Stuffing

Jo Ann

2 c. cooked turkey, cubed
4 c. assorted vegetables,
  cooked and sliced into
  bite-size pieces
10-3/4 oz. can cream of
  celery soup
10-3/4 oz. can cream of
  potato soup
1 c. milk
1/4 t. dried thyme
1/8 t. pepper
4 c. prepared sage-flavored
  stuffing mix

Arrange turkey in an ungreased shallow 3-quart casserole dish; top with vegetables. Stir together soups, milk, thyme and pepper in a bowl; spread over turkey and vegetables. Top with stuffing. Bake at 400 degrees for 25 minutes, until hot. Makes 4 to 6 servings.

Shrimp & Feta Casserole

Jill Valentine, Jackson, TN

2 eggs
1 c. evaporated milk
1 c. plain yogurt
3-oz. pkg. crumbled feta
  cheese
2 c. shredded Swiss cheese
1/4 c. fresh parsley,
  chopped
1 t. dried basil
1 t. dried oregano
4 cloves garlic, minced
8-oz. pkg. angel hair pasta,
  cooked
16-oz. jar chunky salsa
1 lb. medium shrimp,
  peeled, cleaned and
  divided
8-oz. pkg. shredded
  mozzarella cheese

In a medium bowl, combine the first 9 ingredients; set aside. Spread half the pasta in a greased 13"x9" baking pan. Cover with salsa; add half the shrimp. Spread remaining pasta over shrimp; top with egg mixture. Add remaining shrimp and top with mozzarella cheese. Bake at 350 degrees for 30 minutes. Remove from oven and let stand for 5 minutes before serving. Serves 6 to 8.

Quick tip

Oh-so-easy iced tea...perfect with dinner anytime. Fill a 2-quart pitcher with water and drop in 6 to 8 tea bags. Refrigerate overnight. Discard tea bags; add sugar to taste and serve over ice.

Homestyle Turkey & Stuffing

Simple Turkey Pot Pie

Party Ham Casserole
Jill Williams, Hiawatha, KS

6 T. butter, divided
1/4 c. all-purpose flour
2 c. milk
1 c. American cheese, shredded
1/4 c. slivered blanched almonds
3 to 4 potatoes, cooked and sliced
14-1/2 oz. can green beans, drained
2 c. smoked ham, cubed
1-1/2 c. soft bread crumbs

Melt 4 tablespoons butter in a saucepan over low heat; stir in flour. Gradually add milk, stirring constantly until thickened. Add cheese; heat slowly until melted. Stir in almonds; set aside. Arrange potato slices in a greased 2-quart casserole dish; top with green beans. Pour half of cheese mixture over green beans; top with ham and remaining cheese mixture. Melt remaining butter and toss with bread crumbs; sprinkle crumbs over casserole. Bake at 350 degrees for 30 to 35 minutes, or until crumbs are lightly golden. Serves 6 to 8.

Rotini-Tuna Casserole
Tammy Rowe, Bellevue, OH

10-3/4 oz. can cream of chicken soup
1-1/4 c. milk
16-oz. pkg. rainbow rotini pasta, cooked
14-1/2 oz. can mixed vegetables, drained
6-oz. can tuna, drained
8-oz. can sliced mushrooms, drained
2-oz. jar pimentos, drained
salt and pepper to taste
1 t. dried parsley
1/2 c. shredded Cheddar cheese
1/2 c. potato chips, crushed

In a large bowl, mix soup and milk together. Add pasta, vegetables, tuna, mushrooms, pimentos and seasonings; mix well. Pour into an ungreased 2-quart casserole dish; top with cheese and potato chip crumbs. Bake at 350 degrees for 30 minutes, or until heated through. Serves 6 to 8.

Simple Turkey Pot Pie
Cathy Rutz, Andover, KS

16-oz. pkg. frozen mixed vegetables, thawed and drained
2 14-3/4 oz. cans creamed corn
10-3/4 oz. can cream of mushroom soup
3/4 c. milk
2 c. cooked turkey, chopped
2 12-oz. tubes refrigerated buttermilk biscuits, quartered

Mix vegetables, corn, soup, milk and turkey; pour into a 13"x9" baking pan sprayed with non-stick vegetable spray. Top with biscuits; bake at 350 degrees for 35 to 40 minutes, or until biscuits are golden. Serves 6.

Quick tip

Make your own dry bread crumbs...a terrific way to use day-old bread. Dry out bread slices in a 250-degree oven, then tear into sections and pulse in your food processor or blender.

Zucchini Boats

Audrey Piatti, Leonardo, NJ

1 lb. ground beef
1 onion, chopped
16-oz. jar spaghetti sauce
2 large zucchini, halved
  lengthwise
salt and pepper to taste
1/2 c. grated Parmesan
  cheese
1 c. shredded mozzarella
  cheese

Brown beef and onion in a skillet over medium heat; drain. Add spaghetti sauce to beef mixture and stir until combined. Meanwhile, lay zucchini halves, cut-side down, on a microwave-safe plate. Cook on high setting until fork-tender, about 5 to 10 minutes. Scoop out seeds and some surrounding pulp; discard. Sprinkle zucchini halves with salt and pepper; place in a greased 13"x9" baking pan. Spoon beef mixture into hollowed-out zucchini halves and top with cheeses. Bake, uncovered, at 350 degrees for about 40 minutes, or until heated through and cheese is bubbly. Serves 4.

Zucchini Boats

Bavarian Beef & Noodles

Janie Branstetter, Duncan, OK

8-oz. pkg. egg dumpling
  noodles, uncooked
1 lb. ground beef
2 8-oz. cans tomato sauce
1 t. salt
1/4 t. garlic salt
1/8 t. pepper
2 c. sour cream
1/2 c. green onions, sliced
1 c. shredded Cheddar
  cheese

Cook noodles according to package directions; drain and set aside. Meanwhile, brown ground beef in a skillet over medium heat; drain. Stir in tomato sauce, salt, garlic salt and pepper. In a bowl, combine sour cream, onions and noodles. In a greased 2-quart casserole dish, alternate layers of noodle mixture and beef mixture, ending with beef. Sprinkle cheese over top. Bake, uncovered, at 350 degrees for 20 to 25 minutes. Serves 4 to 6.

Quick tip

Whenever just a little onion is needed for a casserole recipe, use green onions instead. Easily cut with kitchen scissors, they add a light onion flavor with no leftover onion to store.

Bavarian Beef & Noodles

Asparagus Shepherd's Pie

Asparagus Shepherd's Pie

Kathy Reichert, Meridian, ID

6 potatoes, peeled and
    quartered
1 lb. ground beef
1 onion, chopped
2 cloves garlic, minced
10-3/4 oz. can cream of
    asparagus soup
1/4 t. pepper
1 lb. asparagus, trimmed
    and cut into 1-inch pieces

1/2 c. milk
1/4 c. butter
1 t. dried sage
3/4 t. salt
1/2 c. shredded mozzarella
    cheese
paprika to taste

Add potatoes to a saucepan; cover with water. Cook over medium heat until tender. Drain and set aside; cover to keep warm. Brown beef in a skillet over medium heat; drain. Add onion and garlic; cook until tender. Stir in soup and pepper. Pour mixture into a greased 2-quart casserole dish. Cook asparagus in a small amount of water over medium heat until crisp-tender, about 3 to 4 minutes. Drain and arrange over beef mixture. Mash potatoes with milk, butter, sage and salt. Spread over asparagus. Sprinkle with cheese and paprika. Bake, uncovered, at 350 degrees for 20 minutes. Makes 4 to 6 servings.

Roasted Veggies & Kielbasa

Carrie Fostor, Baltic, OH

1 lb. Kielbasa sausage,
    sliced into bite-size
    pieces
6 potatoes, peeled and
    chopped
1 c. baby carrots
1 onion, halved and sliced

1 green pepper, cut into
    squares
8-oz. pkg. mushrooms,
    halved
Cajun seasoning to taste

Combine all ingredients in a roaster pan. For a moist consistency, cover before baking; leave uncovered for a dryer consistency. Bake at 425 degrees for 30 minutes, or until vegetables are tender. Makes 8 servings.

Crab-Stuffed Eggplant

Karen Pilcher, Burleson, TX

1-1/2 lb. eggplant
5-1/2 T. butter, divided
1/2 c. dried bread crumbs
1/4 c. grated Parmesan
    cheese
6 to 8 green onions,
    chopped
2 T. fresh parsley, chopped
1 lb. jumbo lump
    crabmeat

1/4 t. salt
1/4 t. pepper
1/2 c. mayonnaise
1 T. all-purpose flour
1/2 c. whipping cream
1 T. Worcestershire sauce

Cover eggplant with water in a saucepan; boil for 15 minutes. Drain. When cool enough to handle, cut in half lengthwise and remove pulp, leaving a shell 1/4-inch thick. Chop pulp and reserve. Arrange shells in a lightly greased 13"x9" baking pan; set aside. Melt one tablespoon butter in a large skillet; add bread crumbs and sauté until golden. Add cheese and stir to coat; set aside. In a separate skillet, melt 4 tablespoons butter. Add green onions and parsley; sauté for 2 minutes. Add eggplant pulp and remaining ingredients, except remaining butter. Sauté eggplant mixture, stirring constantly, for 3 minutes. Spoon filling into each of the shells. Sprinkle with bread crumb mixture; dot with remaining butter. Bake at 400 degrees for 20 minutes. Serves 2 to 4.

Quick tip

Too many zucchini? Grate extra zucchini and freeze it in 2-cup portions...it'll be ready to add to your favorite recipes all winter long.

Ravioli Taco Bake

Margie Kirkman, High Point, NC

1-1/2 lbs. ground beef
1-1/4 oz. pkg. taco
  seasoning mix
3/4 c. water
40-oz. can meat-filled
  ravioli with sauce

8-oz. pkg. shredded
  Cheddar cheese
Optional: sliced black
  olives

Brown ground beef in a large skillet over medium heat; drain. Stir in seasoning mix and water. Reduce heat; simmer for 8 to 10 minutes. Place ravioli in a lightly greased 13"x9" baking pan; spoon beef mixture over top. Sprinkle with cheese. Bake, uncovered, at 350 degrees for 25 to 30 minutes, until cheese is melted and bubbly. If desired, sprinkle with olives before serving. Serves 6 to 8.

Supreme Pizza Casserole

Supreme Pizza Casserole

Tasha Petenzi, Goodlettsville, TN

16-oz. pkg. rotini pasta,
  uncooked
2 15-oz. jars pizza sauce
2-1/4 oz. can sliced black
  olives, drained
4-oz. can sliced
  mushrooms, drained

1 green pepper, chopped
1 onion, chopped
20 to 30 pepperoni slices
2 c. shredded pizza-blend
  or Italian-blend cheese

Cook pasta according to package directions; drain. Combine pasta with remaining ingredients except cheese. Transfer to a 3-quart casserole dish; top with cheese. Bake, uncovered, at 425 degrees for 20 to 25 minutes, until cheese is golden and bubbly. Serves 8 to 10.

Mock Oyster Casserole

Dale Duncan, Waterloo, LA

1 eggplant, peeled and
  sliced into 1-inch cubes
1/2 c. butter, melted
1-1/2 c. buttery round
  cracker crumbs
1 egg, beaten

6-1/2 oz. can minced
  clams, drained and
  liquid reserved
salt, pepper and hot
  pepper sauce to taste

In a saucepan, drop eggplant into boiling water for 3 minutes. Drain well; set aside. Add butter to cracker crumbs; mix well. Reserve 1/3 cup crumb mixture for topping. Gently mix beaten egg, clams and eggplant. Add crumb mixture, salt, pepper and hot pepper sauce. Add just enough reserved clam liquid to make moist, but not soupy. Pour into a greased 11"x7" baking pan. Top with reserved crumbs and bake at 350 degrees for 45 minutes. Serves 4 to 6.

Ravioli Taco Bake

Peg's Tomato-Bacon Pie

Over-Stuffed Shells

Stacy Huntley, League City, Texas.

10-oz. pkg. frozen chopped spinach, thawed and drained
2 c. shredded mozzarella cheese, divided
1 c. cooked ham, diced
2 c. cooked chicken, shredded
15-oz. container ricotta cheese
1/2 c. grated Parmesan cheese
1/2 c. fresh parsley, minced
1-1/2 t. garlic powder
1-1/2 t. onion powder
28-oz. jar Alfredo sauce, divided
12-oz. pkg. jumbo shell pasta, cooked
Garnish: fresh parsley and tomato, chopped

Mix spinach, 1-1/4 cups mozzarella cheese, ham, chicken, ricotta cheese, Parmesan cheese, parsley, garlic and onion powders together; set aside. Spread 2 cups Alfredo sauce into the bottom of an ungreased 13"x9" baking pan; spread one cup sauce into an ungreased 8"x8" baking pan. Spoon 2 tablespoons filling into each pasta shell; arrange shells in a single layer in both pans on top of sauce. Bake, uncovered, at 350 degrees for 30 to 35 minutes; sprinkle with remaining mozzarella cheese. Bake an additional 5 minutes, or until cheese melts. Garnish with parsley and tomato. Serves 6 to 8.

Quick tip

Pop unripe tomatoes into a brown paper grocery bag and store in a dark closet. They'll ripen overnight!

Peg's Tomato-Bacon Pie

Peggy Buckshaw, Stow, OH

2 to 3 tomatoes, sliced
9-inch pie crust, baked
salt and pepper to taste
1/2 c. green onions, chopped
1/3 c. fresh basil, chopped
1/2 c. bacon, crisply cooked and crumbled
1 c. mayonnaise
1 c. shredded Cheddar cheese

Layer tomato slices in pie crust. Season to taste with salt and pepper. Top with onions, basil and bacon. In a bowl, mix together mayonnaise and cheese; spread over bacon. Bake, uncovered, at 350 degrees for 30 minutes, or until lightly golden. Serves 6 to 8.

Over-Stuffed Shells

Delicious Dinners

Parmesan Salmon Bake with Penne

Karen McCann, Marion, OH

16-oz. pkg. penne pasta, uncooked
10 T. butter, divided
2 c. half-and-half
1/2 c. grated Parmesan cheese
1/4 t. nutmeg
salt and pepper to taste
15-oz. can salmon, drained and flaked, bones and skin removed
1 T. fresh parsley, finely chopped
Garnish: additional grated Parmesan cheese

Cook pasta according to package directions. Drain; transfer pasta to a 13"x9" baking pan coated with one tablespoon butter. Toss pasta with one tablespoon butter to coat well; set aside. Meanwhile, in a saucepan over medium heat, whisk together remaining butter, half-and-half, cheese and nutmeg until sauce thickens. Season with salt and pepper. Pour sauce over pasta; add salmon and parsley and mix well. Bake, uncovered, at 425 degrees for 15 to 20 minutes, until hot and bubbly. Serve with additional Parmesan cheese. Makes 8 servings.

Quick tip

Jot down favorite recipes, ones that have been handed down, and make copies to share when family & friends are together. It's a terrific way to preserve those that are time-tested and bring back the sweetest memories.

Western Round-Up

Kay Marone, Des Moines, IA

1 lb. ground beef
2 red peppers, cut into 2-inch squares
1/4 c. onion, chopped
15-oz. can baked beans
1 T. fajita seasoning
8-1/2 oz. pkg. cornbread mix
1 egg, beaten
1/3 c. milk

Combine ground beef, peppers and onion in a large oven-safe skillet over medium-high heat; cook and stir until beef is browned and onion is translucent. Drain. Add beans and fajita seasoning; heat through, stirring frequently. Spread out evenly in skillet; set aside. Mix cornbread with egg and milk according to package directions. Spread evenly over ground beef mixture in skillet; place skillet in the oven. Bake at 350 degrees for 20 minutes, or until a toothpick inserted into cornbread layer comes out clean. Let cool slightly before serving; cut into wedges. Serves 6.

Baked Chicken Chow Mein

Judi Leaming, Dover, DE

10-3/4 oz. can cream of chicken soup
10-3/4 oz. can cream of celery soup
5-oz. can evaporated milk
4-oz. can mushroom stems and pieces, drained
8-oz. can water chestnuts, drained and chopped
2 c. cooked chicken, cubed
5-oz. can chow mein noodles, divided
2 t. Worcestershire sauce
1 to 2 t. curry powder
2 T. butter

In a bowl, combine soups and milk; fold in mushrooms, water chestnuts, chicken and half the chow mein noodles. Sprinkle with Worcestershire sauce and curry powder; stir to combine. Spread into a greased 2-quart casserole dish. Top with remaining noodles; dot with butter. Bake, uncovered, at 350 degrees for 30 minutes, or until bubbly. Serves 4 to 6.

Baked Chicken Chow Mein

Quick Beefy Bean & Biscuit Bake

Quick Beefy Bean & Biscuit Bake

Hana Brosmer, Huntingburg, IN

1 lb. ground beef
1/2 c. onion, chopped
1 t. salt
1/2 t. pepper
28-oz. can brown sugar
  baked beans
1/4 c. barbecue sauce
1/4 c. catsup
1 c. shredded Cheddar
  cheese
16.3-oz. tube refrigerated
  buttermilk biscuits

In a skillet over medium heat, brown beef with onion, salt and pepper; drain. Stir in baked beans, barbecue sauce and catsup; spoon beef mixture into an ungreased 3-quart casserole dish. Sprinkle cheese evenly over top. Separate each biscuit into 2 thinner biscuits and arrange evenly on top. Bake, uncovered, at 350 degrees for 30 to 35 minutes, until bubbly and biscuits are golden. Makes 6 to 8 servings.

Famous Calico Beans

Turkey & Wild Rice Quiche

Angela Biggin, Lyons, IL

1 c. wild rice, uncooked
1/3 c. green onions,
  chopped
1/4 c. red pepper, chopped
5 T. butter
10-inch deep-dish pie
  crust
1/2 lb. deli smoked turkey,
  diced
2 c. shredded Swiss cheese
6 eggs, beaten
1 c. half-and-half
1 T. Worcestershire sauce

Cook rice according to package directions; set aside. Sauté onions and red pepper in butter over medium heat until crisp-tender. In pie crust, layer turkey, onion mixture, cheese and rice. In a bowl, whisk together remaining ingredients; pour over rice. Bake, uncovered, at 400 degrees for 20 minutes. Reduce heat to 325 degrees and bake an additional 30 to 35 minutes. Remove from oven; let stand 15 minutes before cutting into wedges. Serves 6 to 8.

Famous Calico Beans

Barbara Harman, Petersburg, WV

1 lb. ground beef
1/4 lb. bacon, chopped
1 onion, chopped
16-oz. can pork & beans
15-oz. can kidney beans,
  drained and liquid
  reserved
15-oz. can butter beans,
  drained and liquid
  reserved
1/2 c. catsup
1/2 c. brown sugar, packed
2 T. vinegar
1/2 t. salt

Brown beef, bacon and onion in a large skillet over medium heat; drain. Spread beans in a lightly greased 3-quart casserole dish; add beef mixture. In a bowl, combine remaining ingredients; pour over beef mixture. If more liquid is needed, add reserved liquid from beans. Bake, uncovered, at 350 degrees for one hour. Serves 8.

Autumn Pork Chop Bake

Quick tip

For a crispy, crunchy casserole topping, leave the casserole dish uncovered while it's baking. Cover it if you prefer a softer consistency.

Daddy's Shepherd's Pie

Sheila Wakeman, Winnsboro, TX

1 lb. ground beef

10-3/4 oz. can cream of mushroom soup

2/3 c. water

7.2-oz. pkg. homestyle creamy butter-flavored instant mashed potato flakes

2 c. corn

8-oz. pkg. shredded Cheddar cheese

Brown beef in a skillet over medium heat; drain. Stir in soup and water; simmer until heated through. Meanwhile, prepare potato flakes as package directs; set aside. Place beef mixture in a 3-quart casserole dish sprayed with non-stick vegetable spray. Top with corn; spread potatoes evenly across top. Sprinkle with cheese. Bake, uncovered, at 425 degrees for about 10 minutes, or until hot and cheese is melted. Makes 6 to 8 servings.

Autumn Pork Chop Bake

Elizabeth Gilvin, Lexington, KY

14-1/2 oz. can cream of celery soup

1-1/2 c. herb-flavored stuffing mix

1/2 c. corn

1/4 c. celery, chopped

4 boneless pork chops

1 t. brown sugar, packed

1 t. spicy brown mustard

In a bowl, combine soup, stuffing mix, corn and celery. Spoon into a greased 9" pie plate. Top with pork chops. In a bowl, mix together brown sugar and mustard; spoon over pork chops. Bake, uncovered, at 400 degrees for 30 minutes, or until hot and pork chops are cooked through. Serves 4.

Daddy's Shepherd's Pie

Shipwreck Casserole

Shipwreck Casserole

Janis Parr, Ontario, Canada

1 lbs. lean ground beef
1/4 t. salt
1/4 t. pepper
4 potatoes, peeled and
    sliced
1 onion, chopped
8-oz. can pork & beans
10-3/4 oz. can tomato soup

In a skillet over medium heat, brown beef with salt and pepper; drain and set aside. Place potatoes in a greased 2-quart casserole dish; top with onion. Cover with beef mixture. Spoon pork & beans over beef, then pour tomato soup over all. Bake, covered, at 375 degrees for one hour, or until potatoes are tender and casserole is bubbly. Serves 6 to 8.

Beef Burgundy

Melia Himich, Manchester, MI

1-1/2 lbs. beef sirloin,
    cubed
2 1-1/2 oz. pkgs. onion
    soup mix
2 10-3/4 oz. cans cream of
    mushroom soup
1/2 c. burgundy wine or
    beef broth
1/2 c. water
cooked rice or egg noodles

Combine all ingredients except rice or noodles in a Dutch oven. Bake, covered, at 325 degrees for 2-1/2 hours, or until bubbly and beef is cooked through. Serve beef mixture over rice or noodles. Makes 6 to 8 servings.

Quick tip

If you use lots of Italian seasoning, mix up your own to store in a shaker jar...you may already have the ingredients in your spice rack. A good basic blend is 2 tablespoons each of dried oregano, basil, thyme, marjoram and rosemary. Add or subtract to suit your taste.

Beef Burgundy

Italian Pie

Becky Hawkins, Spearfish, SD

1 lb. ground beef
garlic salt and pepper to
    taste
16-oz. jar spaghetti sauce
2 8-oz. tubes refrigerated
    crescent rolls
1/2 c. shredded mozzarella
    cheese
1/2 c. shredded Colby
    cheese

Season beef with garlic salt and pepper to taste; brown in a skillet over medium heat. Drain; add spaghetti sauce to beef and simmer for 5 minutes. Layer one tube of crescent rolls in the bottom of a greased 3-quart casserole dish; spread rolls to edges of pan. Spoon beef mixture over rolls; layer cheeses on top. Spread remaining crescent rolls over cheese layer; cover with aluminum foil. Bake at 350 degrees for 30 minutes. Remove foil and bake 15 more minutes, or until golden. Makes 12 servings.

Delicious Dinners

Alabama Chicken Casserole

Betty Lou Wright, Hendersonville, TN

2 to 3 c. cooked chicken, chopped
4 eggs, hard-boiled, peeled and chopped
2 c. cooked rice
1-1/2 c. celery, chopped
1 onion, chopped
2 10-3/4 oz. cans cream of mushroom soup
1 c. mayonnaise
2 T. lemon juice
3-oz. pkg. slivered almonds
5-oz. can chow mein noodles

Mix all ingredients except noodles in a large bowl. Transfer to a greased 3-quart casserole dish. Cover and refrigerate overnight. Uncover and bake at 350 degrees for one hour, or until hot and bubbly. Top with noodles; return to oven for 5 minutes. Makes 10 to 12 servings.

Alabama Chicken Casserole

Hearty Tortilla Casserole

Angela Murphy, Tempe, AZ

2 lbs. ground beef
1 onion, chopped
2 t. instant coffee granules
1 t. salt
1 t. pepper
1 T. chili powder
29-oz. can tomato sauce, divided
12 10-inch flour tortillas
1/2 c. cream cheese, softened
1/3 c. water
2 c. shredded Cheddar or mozzarella cheese
12 black olives, sliced

Brown beef and onion in a skillet over medium heat; drain. Add coffee granules, seasonings and half the tomato sauce to beef mixture; set aside. Spread each tortilla with cream cheese. Add 1/4 cup of beef mixture to each tortilla and fold over. Place folded tortillas in a greased 3-quart caserole dish. Top with any remaining beef mixture. In a bowl, combine water and remaining tomato sauce; drizzle over tortillas. Sprinkle cheese and olives on top. Cover with aluminum foil and bake at 375 degrees for about 25 minutes, until heated through. Serves 6 to 8.

Hearty Tortilla Casserole

Cowpoke Casserole

Cowpoke Casserole

Debbie Hutchinson, Spring, TX

1 lb. ground beef
1/2 onion, chopped
salt and pepper to taste
1 t. chili powder
15-1/2 oz. can chili beans
8-oz. can tomato sauce
1/2 c. water
8-1/2 oz. pkg. cornbread mix
1/3 c. milk
1 egg, beaten

Brown beef with onion in an oven-proof skillet over medium heat. Drain; add salt and pepper to taste. Stir in chili powder, beans, tomato sauce and water. Simmer for 5 minutes; remove from heat. In a separate bowl, stir together cornbread mix, milk and egg; spoon over beef mixture and place skillet in oven. Bake, uncovered, at 350 degrees for 25 minutes, or until cornbread topping is golden and cooked through. Serves 4 to 6.

Sloppy Joe Casserole

Sloppy Joe Casserole

Amy Hunt, Traphill, NC

1 lb. ground beef
1 onion, diced
1 green pepper, diced
salt to taste
10-3/4 oz. can tomato soup
1/2 c. water
1 t. Worcestershire sauce
7-1/2 oz. tube refrigerated biscuits
1/2 c. shredded Cheddar cheese

Brown beef with onion, pepper and salt in a skillet over medium heat; drain. Stir in soup, water and Worcestershire sauce; heat to a boil. Spoon beef mixture into a greased 1-1/2 quart casserole dish. Arrange biscuits on top of beef mixture around the edges of the dish. Bake, uncovered, at 400 degrees for 15 minutes, or until biscuits are golden. Sprinkle cheese over biscuits; bake again for 15 minutes, or until cheese is melted. Serves 4.

Deep Sea Delight

Carrie O'Shea, Marina Del Rey, CA

3 T. plus 1-1/2 t. butter, divided
1 c. onion, chopped
1-1/2 c. celery, chopped
2-1/2 c. milk
6 T. all-purpose flour
1/4 lb. Cheddar cheese, sliced
1/2 t. salt
1/2 t. pepper
1/4 lb. crabmeat, flaked
1/4 lb. lobster, flaked
1/4 lb. medium shrimp, peeled and cleaned
1/4 lb. scallops

Melt 3 tablespoons butter in a skillet; sauté onion and celery until tender. Set aside. Heat milk in a saucepan over medium heat. Mix in flour and remaining butter until well blended. Gradually blend cheese into mixture; add salt and pepper. In a medium bowl, combine onion mixture with cheese sauce mixture. Toss in seafood; transfer to a greased 11"x7" baking pan. Bake at 350 degrees for 25 minutes, or until seafood is opaque and surface is lightly golden. Serves 4.

Crescent Roll Lasagna
Faith Bedard, Hallock, MN

1-1/2 lbs. ground beef
1 onion, diced
salt and pepper to taste
15-oz. can tomato sauce
1 T. Worcestershire sauce
1/2 t. garlic salt
1 t. Italian seasoning, divided

2 T. brown sugar, packed
2 c. shredded Cheddar cheese
2 c. shredded mozzarella cheese
2 8-oz. tubes refrigerated crescent rolls
8-oz. container sour cream

In a skillet over medium heat, brown beef, onion, salt and pepper; drain. Add sauces, garlic salt, 1/2 teaspoon Italian seasoning and brown sugar. Transfer to a greased 3-quart casserole dish. Top with cheeses. Unroll crescent rolls; spread with about a tablespoon of sour cream and sprinkle with remaining Italian seasoning. Roll up crescent rolls; place on top of cheese. Bake, uncovered, at 350 degrees for 35 to 40 minutes, until bubbly and rolls are golden. Serves 6 to 8.

Crescent Roll Lasagna

Hearty Stuffed Pepper Casserole,
Vickie

2-1/2 c. herb-flavored stuffing mix, divided
1 T. butter, melted
1 lb. ground beef
1/2 c. onion, chopped
14-1/2 oz. can whole tomatoes, chopped

8-oz. can corn, drained
salt and pepper to taste
2 green peppers, quartered

Mix together 1/4 cup dry stuffing mix and butter; set aside. Brown beef and onion in a skillet over medium-high heat; drain. Stir in tomatoes, corn, salt and pepper; add remaining stuffing mix. Arrange green peppers in an ungreased 2-quart casserole dish; spoon beef mixture over top. Cover and bake at 400 degrees for 25 minutes. Sprinkle with reserved stuffing mixture. Bake, uncovered, for 5 additional minutes, or until peppers are tender. Serves 4 to 6.

Hearty Stuffed Pepper Casserole

Blue-Ribbon Corn Dog Bake

Crustless Pizza Quiche
Amy Hunt, Traphill, NC

1/2 c. pepperoni, diced
8-oz. can sliced
   mushrooms, drained
5 eggs, beaten
3/4 c. milk
1/8 t. dried oregano
1/8 t. dried basil
8-oz. pkg. shredded
   mozzarella cheese

Layer pepperoni and mushrooms in a greased 9" pie plate. In a bowl, whisk together eggs, milk and seasoning; pour over pepperoni and mushrooms. Top with cheese. Bake, uncovered, at 400 degrees for 20 to 25 minutes, until golden and heated through. Serves 4 to 6.

Crustless Pizza Quiche

Blue-Ribbon Corn Dog Bake
Tiffani Schulte, Wyandotte, MI

1/3 c. sugar
1 egg, beaten
1 c. all-purpose flour
3/4 T. baking powder
1/2 t. salt
1/2 c. yellow cornmeal
1/2 T. butter, melted
3/4 c. milk
16-oz. pkg. hot dogs, sliced
   into bite-size pieces

In a small bowl, mix together sugar and egg. In a separate bowl, mix together flour, baking powder and salt. Add flour mixture to sugar mixture. Add cornmeal, butter and milk, stirring just to combine. Fold in hot dog pieces. Pour into a well-greased 1-1/2 quart casserole dish. Bake, uncovered, at 375 degrees for about 15 minutes, or until a toothpick inserted near the center comes out clean. Serves 6.

Mom's Texas Hash
Ginger O'Connell, Hazel Park, MI

1 lb. ground beef
2 onions, sliced
1 green pepper, chopped
1 c. stewed tomatoes
1/2 to 1 t. chili powder
1 t. salt

Brown beef, onions and green pepper in a skillet over medium heat; drain. Stir in tomatoes with juice and seasonings. Cook over medium heat until warmed through, about 8 minutes; spoon into an ungreased one-quart casserole dish. Bake, uncovered, at 350 degrees for 15 to 20 minutes. Serves 4.

Chapter 5

Recipes to Feed a Crowd

Potlucks, parties, tailgating and get-togethers all need recipes to fill lots of hungry tummies. You'll find big-batch recipes for everything from breakfast and brunch to dinner and dessert. Looking for the perfect recipe to take to a church supper? You might want to try the Sour Cream-Chicken Enchiladas...they're sure to be a hit!

Sweet Mini Apple Dumplings

Sweet Mini Apple Dumplings

Karen Norman, Jacksonville, FL

2 8-oz. tubes refrigerated
   crescent rolls, separated
4 apples, peeled, cored and
   sliced into 8 wedges
1/2 c. butter
1 c. sugar
1 c. water
1/2 t. cinnamon

Cut each crescent roll in half, forming 2 triangles from each; roll up one apple wedge in each triangle crescent-roll style. Arrange in a 13"x9" baking pan coated with non-stick vegetable spray; set aside. Add butter, sugar and water to a small saucepan; bring to a boil. Reduce heat; boil and stir until sugar dissolves. Pour over crescents; bake at 350 degrees for 30 minutes. Sprinkle with cinnamon. Makes 32 dumplings.

Sweet Corn & Rice Casserole

Linda Stone, Algood, TN

2 T. butter
1 green pepper, chopped
1 onion, chopped
15-1/2 oz. can creamed
   corn
11-oz. can sweet corn &
   diced peppers, drained
11-oz. can corn, drained
10-oz. can diced
   tomatoes with green
   chiles, drained
6 c. cooked rice
8-oz. pkg. mild Mexican
   pasteurized process
   cheese spread, cubed
1/2 t. salt
1/4 t. pepper
1/2 c. shredded Cheddar
   cheese

Melt butter in a large skillet over medium heat. Add green pepper and onion; sauté 5 minutes, or until tender. Stir in remaining ingredients except shredded cheese; spoon into a lightly greased 13"x9" baking pan. Bake, uncovered, at 350 degrees for 25 to 30 minutes, until heated through. Top with shredded cheese; bake an additional 5 minutes, until cheese melts. Makes 10 to 12 servings.

Sweet Corn & Rice Casserole

Peanut Butter Apple Crisp

Linda Belon, Wintersville, OH

1 c. all-purpose flour
1-1/2 c. brown sugar,
   packed
1 t. cinnamon
3/4 c. creamy peanut
   butter
1/3 c. butter, softened
6 to 8 tart apples, peeled,
   cored and thinly sliced
2 T. lemon juice
1 t. lemon zest
Garnish: vanilla ice cream

Combine flour, brown sugar and cinnamon in a bowl. Cut in peanut butter and butter until mixture resembles coarse crumbs; set aside. Arrange apple slices in a lightly greased 3-quart casserole dish; sprinkle with lemon juice and zest. Top apples with crumb mixture. Bake at 350 degrees for 35 to 45 minutes. Serve warm, topped with a scoop of ice cream. Serves 10 to 12.

Cheesy Chicken & Noodles

April Bash, Carlisle, PA

12-oz. pkg. wide egg
noodles, cooked
2 c. cooked chicken, cubed
or shredded
2 10-3/4 oz. cans chicken
noodle soup
10-3/4 oz. can cream of
chicken soup

2 eggs, beaten
2 c. shredded Cheddar
cheese
1 c. seasoned dry bread
crumbs
1 t. garlic salt
1 t. onion salt
salt and pepper to taste

Combine all ingredients in a large bowl; mix well.
Transfer to a lightly greased 13"x9" baking pan. Bake,
uncovered, at 350 degrees for 35 to 40 minutes. Serves
8 to 10.

Cheesy Chicken & Noodles

Chow Mein Noodle Casserole

Vicki Cox, Bland, MO

2 lbs. ground beef
1 onion, chopped
10-3/4 oz. can cream of
celery soup
10-3/4 oz. can golden
mushroom soup
1-1/4 c. water

1/2 t. salt
1 c. instant rice, uncooked
1 T. Worcestershire sauce
1 t. garlic powder
5-oz. can chow mein
noodles

Brown ground beef and onion in a large skillet over
medium heat; drain. Stir together remaining ingredients
except chow mein noodles in a large bowl. Add
beef mixture; mix well. Transfer to a lightly greased
13"x9" baking pan. Bake, uncovered, at 375 degrees
for 20 minutes, until bubbly. Sprinkle with chow
mein noodles; bake, uncovered, for an additional 5 to
10 minutes. Makes 16 servings.

Warm Apple Wraps

Sandy Rowe, Bellevue, OH

21-oz. can apple pie filling
6 8-inch flour tortillas
1 t. cinnamon
1/3 c. butter

1/2 c. sugar
1/2 c. brown sugar, packed
1/2 c. water

Spoon pie filling evenly down the center of each tortilla;
sprinkle with cinnamon. Roll up; place seam-side down
in a lightly buttered 8"x8" baking pan. Set aside. Add
remaining ingredients to a saucepan; bring to a boil.
Reduce heat; simmer and stir for 3 minutes. Pour over
tortillas; bake at 350 degrees for 20 minutes. Slice each
in half and spoon juices on top before serving. Makes
12 servings.

Chow Mein Noodle Casserole

Spinach & Black Bean Lasagna

Spinach & Black Bean Lasagna
Michele Bartolomea, Stafford, VA

2 eggs, beaten
16-oz. container ricotta cheese
10-oz. frozen spinach, thawed and drained
1/2 t. salt
1/4 c. fresh cilantro, chopped
2 c. shredded Monterey Jack cheese
2 c. shredded Pepper Jack cheese
2 16-oz. cans black beans, drained and rinsed
2 13-oz. jars spaghetti sauce
1/2 t. ground cumin
12 strips no-boil lasagna, uncooked

Mix eggs, ricotta cheese, spinach, salt and cilantro in a medium bowl; set aside. In a second bowl, combine Monterey Jack and Pepper Jack cheeses. Set aside. Mash beans with sauce and cumin in a third bowl; mix well. In a lightly greased 13"x9" baking pan, layer lasagna alternately with spinach mixture, cheese mixture and bean mixture, ending with remaining lasagna. Cover with aluminum foil and bake at 350 degrees for 45 minutes. Serves 9 to 12.

Uncle Ed's Baked Beans
Sheri Kohl, Wentzville, MO

3 16-oz. cans pork & beans
1/2 c. bacon, crisply cooked and crumbled
1/3 c. catsup
3 T. molasses
3 T. honey
2 t. onion, chopped
1-1/2 t. mustard
1 t. smoke-flavored cooking sauce
1/2 t. garlic salt
1/4 t. pepper

Combine all ingredients in a lightly greased 1-1/2 quart casserole dish. Stir gently. Bake, uncovered, at 325 degrees for 90 minutes. Makes 10 servings.

Chicken & Spaghetti Casserole
Nadine Rush, London, KY

5 to 6 boneless, skinless chicken breasts
2 to 3 stalks celery, diced
1 onion, diced
salt and pepper to taste
16-oz. pkg. spaghetti, uncooked and broken in half
2 10-3/4 oz. cans cream of chicken soup
8 slices pasteurized process cheese spread
10-oz. pkg. shredded mozzarella cheese

In a large soup pot, combine chicken, celery, onion, salt and pepper; cover with water. Bring to a boil over medium-high heat. Reduce heat to low; simmer until chicken is tender, 30 to 45 minutes. Remove chicken to a plate, reserving broth, celery and onion in soup pot. Bring broth to a boil. Add spaghetti and cook until tender, 8 to 10 minutes; drain. Meanwhile, shred chicken. Combine chicken and soup in a large bowl; transfer to a greased deep 13"x9" glass baking pan. Spoon spaghetti mixture over chicken mixture. Arrange cheese slices on top; sprinkle with shredded cheese. Bake, uncovered, at 350 degrees for 25 minutes, or just until cheese melts and turns golden. Serves 12.

Quick tip
Make a frosty pitcher of strawberry lemonade. Combine a 12-ounce can of frozen lemonade concentrate, a 10-ounce package of frozen strawberries and 4-1/2 cups of cold water. Let stand until berries thaw, then stir well.

Sugared Sweet Potatoes

Patricia Rozzelle, Mineral Bluff, GA

1-1/2 c. brown sugar, packed	1 t. vanilla extract
1/4 c. margarine	1 c. cola
3/4 t. salt	9 sweet potatoes, boiled and sliced

In a medium saucepan, cook brown sugar, margarine, salt, vanilla and cola; bring to a boil for 5 minutes. Arrange potatoes in an ungreased 13"x9" baking pan. Pour brown sugar mixture over potatoes. Bake, uncovered, at 350 degrees for 25 to 30 minutes until edges are crisp. Makes 10 to 12 servings.

Sugared Sweet Potatoes

Aunt Myrtle's Baked Beans

Lucie Wills, Ontario, Canada

1/2 lb. bacon	1 c. brown sugar, packed
1 onion, chopped	1/2 c. catsup
15-oz. can kidney beans	2 T. vinegar
15-oz. can butter beans	1/8 t. garlic powder
2 20-oz. cans pork & beans	

In a skillet over medium-high heat, cook bacon and onion together until bacon is crisp. Drain and reserve drippings. Combine remaining ingredients; stir in bacon, onion and drippings. Spoon into a greased roaster and bake, uncovered, at 350 degrees for 2 hours. Serves 10 to 12.

Sunday Chicken & Dressing

Laura Strausberger, Roswell, GA

10-3/4 oz. can cream of chicken soup	2-1/2 to 3 lbs. cooked chicken, cubed
10-3/4 oz. can cream of celery or cream of mushroom soup	2 6-oz. pkgs. chicken-flavored stuffing mix, prepared
1 c. chicken broth	

Combine soups and broth in a large bowl; set aside. Place half of chicken in a lightly greased 13"x9" baking pan; top with half of stuffing and half of soup mixture. Repeat layers, ending with soup mixture. Bake, uncovered, at 350 degrees for one hour. Makes 10 servings.

Aunt Myrtle's Baked Beans

French Toast Berry Bake

French Toast Berry Bake

Suzanne Vella, Babylon, NY

12 slices French bread,
   sliced 1-inch thick

5 eggs, beaten

2-1/2 c. milk

1-3/4 c. brown sugar,
   packed and divided

1-1/2 t. vanilla extract

1-1/4 t. cinnamon

Optional: 1/2 t. nutmeg,
   1/4 t. ground cloves

Optional: 1 c. chopped
   pecans

1/2 c. butter, melted

2 c. blueberries,
   strawberries, raspberries
   and/or blackberries

Arrange bread slices in a greased 13"x9" baking pan; set aside. In a bowl, combine eggs, milk, one cup brown sugar, vanilla, cinnamon and desired spices. Whisk until blended; pour over bread. Cover and refrigerate for 8 hours to overnight. Let stand at room temperature 30 minutes before baking. Sprinkle with pecans, if using. Combine melted butter and remaining brown sugar; drizzle over top. Bake, uncovered, at 400 degrees for 30 minutes. Sprinkle with berries and bake an additional 10 minutes, or until a fork comes out clean. Serves 12.

Cabbage Roll Casserole

Cabbage Roll Casserole

Dianne Gregory, Sheridan, AR

2 lbs. ground beef,
   browned

1 c. onion, chopped

29-oz. can tomato sauce

1 head cabbage, chopped

1 c. instant rice, uncooked

1 t. salt

14-oz. can beef broth

Combine all ingredients except broth in an ungreased, deep 13"x9" baking pan. Drizzle with broth; cover with aluminum foil. Bake at 350 degrees for one hour; uncover and stir. Cover again; bake 30 additional minutes, or until rice is cooked and casserole is heated through. Makes 10 to 12 servings.

Quick tip

Food for friends doesn't have to be fancy... your guests will be thrilled with old-fashioned comfort foods. Let everyone help themselves from big platters set right on the table. They'll love it!

Add chicken, mayonnaise, soup and salt; mix well. Melt remaining butter and toss with cereal; sprinkle over top. Bake, uncovered, at 350 degrees for 30 minutes. Makes 10 servings.

Lasagna Florentine
Diane Cohen, Kennesaw, GA

1 lb. ground beef
1/2 c. onion, chopped
2 to 3 cloves garlic, minced
26-oz. jar spaghetti sauce, divided
16-oz. container cottage cheese
10-oz. pkg. frozen spinach, thawed and drained

12-oz. pkg. shredded mozzarella cheese, divided
1/2 c. grated Parmesan cheese, divided
2 eggs, beaten
9 lasagna noodles, cooked

Brown ground beef, onion and garlic. Drain; stir in spaghetti sauce and set aside. In a large bowl, combine cottage cheese, spinach, 2 cups mozzarella cheese, 1/4 cup Parmesan cheese and eggs. In an ungreased 13"x9" baking pan, layer one cup sauce mixture, 3 noodles and 1/2 cup cottage cheese mixture; repeat layering once. Top with remaining 3 noodles, sauce mixture, mozzarella and Parmesan. Cover with aluminum foil; bake at 350 degrees for 30 minutes. Uncover; bake for an additional 15 minutes. Let stand for 10 minutes before serving. Makes 9 servings.

Lasagna Florentine

Crunchy Hot Chicken Salad
Lynne Davisson, Cable, OH

6 T. butter, divided
1 c. celery, chopped
1/2 c. green pepper, diced
1/3 c. onion, chopped
2 to 3 T. diced pimentos
4-oz. can sliced mushrooms, drained
2-1/4 oz. pkg. slivered almonds

4 c. cooked chicken, diced
1 c. mayonnaise
10-3/4 oz. can cream of celery soup
1 t. salt
1 c. corn flake cereal, crushed

Melt 4 tablespoons butter in a large skillet over medium heat; add vegetables and almonds. Sauté until vegetables are tender; spoon into an ungreased 13"x9" baking pan.

Quick tip
When making a favorite casserole, why not make a double batch? After baking, let the extra casserole cool, wrap and tuck it in the freezer. It'll be ready to share with a new mother, carry to a potluck or reheat on a busy night at home.

Crunchy Hot Chicken Salad

Friendship Casserole

Friendship Casserole

April King, Eugene, OR

1/2 c. butter
10 eggs
1/2 c. all-purpose flour
1 t. baking powder
1/8 t. salt
7-oz. can chopped green chiles

16-oz. container cottage cheese
2 8-oz. pkgs. shredded Monterey Jack cheese

Melt butter in a 13"x9" baking pan, spreading evenly. Beat eggs in a large bowl; stir in flour, baking powder and salt until well blended. Add melted butter and remaining ingredients; mix just until blended. Pour into pan and bake, uncovered, at 400 degrees for 15 minutes; reduce temperature to 350 degrees. Bake for an additional 35 to 40 minutes. Cut into squares and serve hot. Serves 10 to 12.

Amish Breakfast Casserole

Barb Bargdill, Gooseberry Patch

1 lb. bacon, diced
1 sweet onion, chopped
1 green pepper, diced
10 eggs, beaten
1-1/2 c. cream-style cottage cheese

4 c. frozen shredded hashbrowns, thawed
2 c. shredded Cheddar cheese
1-1/2 c. shredded Monterey Jack cheese, divided

In a large skillet over medium heat, cook bacon, onion and green pepper until bacon is crisp; drain and set aside. In a large bowl, combine remaining ingredients, reserving 1/4 cup of the Monterey Jack cheese. Stir bacon mixture into egg mixture. Transfer to a greased 13"x9" baking pan; sprinkle with reserved cheese. Bake, uncovered, at 350 degrees for 35 to 40 minutes, until set and bubbly. Let stand 10 minutes before cutting. Makes 8 to 10 servings.

Abuela's Garlic Grits

Kelly Petty, Aiken, SC

4-1/2 c. water
1 t. salt
1 c. quick-cooking grits, uncooked
1/2 c. butter, cubed
3/4 lb. pasteurized process cheese spread, cubed

2 eggs, beaten
2/3 c. milk
1/4 t. garlic powder
1 c. wheat & barley cereal nuggets
hot pepper sauce to taste

In a saucepan over high heat, bring water and salt to a boil. Slowly stir in grits; cook 3 to 5 minutes, stirring constantly. Remove from heat. Add butter and cheese, stirring until melted. Beat eggs, milk and garlic powder together; stir into hot mixture. Pour into an ungreased 13"x9" glass baking pan. Sprinkle with cereal and hot sauce. Bake, uncovered, at 350 degrees for one hour. Let stand 15 minutes before serving. Serves 10 to 12.

Amish Breakfast Casserole

Recipes to Feed a Crowd

Garden-Fresh Egg Casserole

Anne Muns, Scottsdale, AZ

1 c. buttermilk
1/2 c. onion, grated
1-1/2 c. shredded Monterey
  Jack cheese
1 c. cottage cheese
1 c. spinach, chopped
1 c. tomatoes, chopped
1/2 c. butter, melted
18 eggs, beaten

Mix all ingredients together; pour into a greased 13"x9" baking pan. Cover; refrigerate overnight. Bake at 350 degrees for 50 minutes to one hour. Serves 8 to 10.

Baked Potato Salad

Kathie Williams, Oakland City, IN

13 to 15 potatoes, cooked
  and cubed
1-1/2 to 2 lbs. bacon,
  crisply cooked and
  crumbled
1 onion, chopped
3 c. shredded Cheddar
  cheese, divided
16-oz. jar mayonnaise-type
  salad dressing

Combine potatoes, bacon, half the cheese, onion and enough salad dressing to make the mixture moist; mix well. Spread into a large roasting pan; sprinkle with remaining cheese. Bake at 350 degrees until bubbly, about one hour. Serves 18 to 20.

Quick tip

Make mini pot pies. Spoon filling into oven-safe bowls and add batter topping, or cut circles of pie crust to fit, using another bowl as a guide. Set on a baking sheet and bake until bubbly and golden...delicious, and everyone gets their own little pot pie!

Cheesy Hashbrowns

Joanne McDonald, British Columbia, Canada

30-oz. pkg. frozen
  shredded hashbrowns,
  thawed
2 c. sour cream
1 onion, chopped
2 10-3/4 oz. cans cream of
  mushroom soup
2 c. shredded Cheddar
  cheese, divided

Combine hashbrowns, sour cream, soup, onion and 2 cups cheese together; mix well. Spread into a lightly buttered 13"x9" baking pan; sprinkle with remaining cheese. Bake at 350 degrees for one hour. Makes 8 to 10 servings.

Baked Potato Salad

Garden-Fresh Egg Casserole

Quiche-Me-Quick

Quiche-Me-Quick

Sandy Bernards, Valencia, CA

1/2 c. butter
1/2 c. all-purpose flour
6 eggs, beaten
1 c. milk
16-oz. pkg. Monterey Jack
   cheese, cubed

3-oz. pkg. cream cheese,
   softened
2 c. cottage cheese
1 t. baking powder
1 t. salt
1 t. sugar

Melt butter in a saucepan; add flour. Cook and stir until smooth; beat in the remaining ingredients. Stir until well blended; pour into a greased 13"x9" baking pan. Bake at 350 degrees for 45 minutes. Serves 10 to 12.

Deep-Dish Taco Squares

Jody Bolen, Ashland, OH

2 c. biscuit baking mix
1/2 c. water
1 lb. ground beef
1 green pepper, chopped
1 onion, chopped
1/8 t. garlic powder
8-oz. can tomato sauce
1-1/4 oz. pkg. taco
   seasoning mix
1 c. shredded Cheddar
   cheese

1 c. sour cream
1/3 c. mayonnaise-type
   salad dressing
1/4 t. paprika
Garnish: sour cream,
   chopped tomatoes,
   chopped lettuce, chopped
   onion

Mix biscuit baking mix and water; spread in lightly greased 13"x9" baking pan. Bake at 375 degrees for 9 minutes; remove from oven and set aside. Brown together ground beef, green pepper, onion and garlic powder; drain and stir in tomato sauce and taco seasoning. Spread mixture over crust. Stir together cheese, sour cream and salad dressing; spoon over beef mixture and sprinkle with paprika. Bake at 375 degrees for an additional 25 minutes. Cut into squares; garnish with sour cream, tomatoes, lettuce and onion. Makes 12 to 15 servings.

Shredded Chicken

Barbara Wise, Jamestown, OH

2 3-lb. cans chicken,
   drained
1 loaf day-old bread, torn
1/2 c. onion, chopped

1 stalk celery, chopped
16-oz. can chicken broth

Mix first 4 ingredients together; add enough chicken broth until the consistency of very thick soup is achieved. Spread into an ungreased 13"x9" baking pan; bake at 350 degrees for 1-1/2 hours. Serves 24.

Shredded Chicken

Green Bean Bake
Jennie Parker, Rochester, NY

5 14-1/2 oz. cans green
   beans, drained
5 slices bacon, diced
1 onion, chopped

1 c. catsup
1 c. brown sugar, packed

Combine ingredients; spread in an ungreased 13"x9"
baking pan. Bake at 250 degrees for 3 hours.
Serves 8 to 10.

3-Bean & Ham Casserole
Melanie Lowe,Dover, DE

10-oz. pkg. frozen lima
   beans, cooked
3 16-oz. cans baked beans,
   drained and rinsed
2 16-oz. cans kidney
   beans, drained and
   rinsed
1 lb. pork sausage links,
   sliced into 2-inch pieces

1/2 lb. smoked ham, cubed
1 T. salt
1-1/2 t. pepper
1/2 t. mustard
8-oz. can tomato sauce
1/2 c. catsup
1/4 c. brown sugar, packed
1 onion, chopped

Combine all ingredients in an ungreased 3-1/2 quart
casserole dish; mix well. Bake, uncovered, at 400 degrees
for one hour. Makes 16 to 20 servings.

Potatoes Romanoff
Sally Borland, Port Gibson, NY

6 to 9 c. potatoes, peeled,
   cooked and cubed
salt to taste
2 c. cottage cheese
1 c. sour cream

1/4 c. onion, minced
garlic powder to taste
1/2 c. shredded Cheddar
   cheese

Sprinkle potatoes with salt. Combine with cottage
cheese, sour cream, onion and garlic powder. Pour
into an ungreased 1-1/2 quart casserole dish. Top with
cheese. Bake at 350 degrees for 40 to 50 minutes. Makes
12 to 14 servings.

Green Bean Bake

Quick tip
Need to accommodate a last-minute
dinner guest? Add a few more veggies and
toppings to your casserole...chances are
good that no one will even notice!

3-Bean & Ham Casserole

Confetti Ziti

Confetti Ziti
Vanessa Longenecker, Lancaster, PA

16-oz. pkg. ziti, cooked
1-1/2 c. red pepper, sliced
1-1/2 c. yellow pepper, sliced
2 c. shredded Cheddar cheese
2 c. shredded Monterey Jack cheese
28-oz. can whole tomatoes
1 t. salt
1 t. pepper
1 c. half-and-half
1/2 c. seasoned dry bread crumbs

Combine ziti, peppers, cheese, tomatoes, salt and pepper in a greased 13"x9" baking pan. Pour half-and-half over the top; cover with aluminum foil. Bake at 350 degrees for 30 minutes; remove cover. Sprinkle with bread crumbs; bake, uncovered, for an additional 30 minutes. Serves 12.

Creamy Broccoli & Cheese
Stella Hickman, Gooseberry Patch

4 10-oz. pkgs. frozen broccoli
1 c. butter, divided
3-1/2 c. corn flake cereal, crushed
12-oz. pkg. cream cheese, cubed and divided
12 slices American cheese

Prepare broccoli according to package directions; drain well and set aside. Melt 1/2 cup butter; toss with cereal and set aside. Stir cream cheese and remaining butter together in a small saucepan over low heat until melted; remove from heat and set aside. Layer half the broccoli in an ungreased 2-quart casserole dish; spread half the cream cheese mixture on top. Arrange 6 slices of cheese on top; sprinkle with half the cereal mixture. Repeat layers one time; bake, uncovered, at 350 degrees for one hour. Makes 12 to 15 servings.

Georgian Cheese Grits
Jason Keller, Carrollton, GA

6 c. water
1-1/2 c. quick-cooking grits, uncooked
3/4 c. butter
16-oz. pkg. pasteurized processed cheese spread, cubed
2 t. seasoned salt
1 T. Worcestershire sauce
1/2 t. hot pepper sauce
3 eggs, beaten

Bring water to a boil in a medium saucepan; stir in grits. Reduce heat to low; cover and cook for 5 to 6 minutes, stirring occasionally. Add butter, cheese, seasoned salt and sauces. Continue cooking and stirring for 5 minutes, until cheese is melted. Remove from heat; let cool slightly and fold in eggs. Pour into a lightly greased 13"x9" baking pan. Bake at 350 degrees for one hour, or until top is golden. Makes 12 servings.

Quick tip

Tile squares make great trivets. Found at any home-improvement store, they come in all shapes, sizes and colors.

Weekend Beef Burgundy

Virginia Watson, Scranton, PA

2 lbs. stew beef, cubed
10-3/4 oz. can cream of
  mushroom soup
1/2 c. onion, chopped
1 t. beef bouillon granules
1-oz. pkg. herb and lemon
  soup mix, divided
4-1/2 oz. can sliced
  mushrooms, drained
1/2 c. Burgundy wine or
  beef broth
4 c. cooked egg noodles

Combine beef, soup, onion and bouillon in a large bowl; mix well. Stir in half the package of soup mix, reserving the rest for another recipe. Spread in a lightly greased 13"x9" baking pan; cover and bake at 325 degrees for 4 hours. Add mushrooms and wine or broth; bake for an additional 10 minutes. Add noodles and stir to combine. Serves 8 to 10.

Baked Zucchini Gratin

Baked Zucchini Gratin

Heather Anne Kehr, Littlestown, PA

1 onion, sliced
2 lbs. zucchini, sliced
1/2 c. butter, melted and
  divided
2 c. shredded mozzarella
  cheese
1/2 c. dry bread crumbs
1/4 c. grated Parmesan
  cheese

In a lightly greased 2-quart casserole dish, layer onion and zucchini. Drizzle with 1/4 cup butter; sprinkle with mozzarella cheese. In a separate bowl, combine remaining butter, bread crumbs and Parmesan cheese. Sprinkle crumb mixture evenly over the top. Bake, uncovered, at 350 degrees for 35 to 40 minutes, until zucchini is tender. Makes 8 servings.

Rice Casserole

Jennifer Harter, Fort Worth, TX

1 c. green pepper, diced
1 c. onion, diced
2 T. butter
3 c. long-cooking rice,
  uncooked
10-oz. pkg. frozen,
  chopped broccoli, thawed
4-oz. can mushroom
  pieces, drained
16-oz. jar pasteurized
  process cheese sauce
2 10-3/4 oz. cans cream
  of mushroom soup

In a medium skillet, sauté pepper and onion with butter. Combine remaining ingredients and onion mixture in a greased 13"x9" baking pan. Bake, covered, at 350 degrees for 30 minutes; uncover, and bake an additional 30 minutes. Makes 10 servings.

Rice Casserole

Recipes to Feed a Crowd

White Lasagna
Molly Ebert, Decatur, IN

8-oz. pkg. lasagna noodles, uncooked
3 T. butter
1 t. lemon juice
16-oz. pkg. sliced mushrooms
1/4 c. all-purpose flour
1 t. salt
1/8 t. cayenne pepper
2-1/2 c. milk
2 T. fresh parsley, chopped
16-oz. container ricotta or cottage cheese
1/2 c. grated Parmesan cheese

Cook lasagna according to package directions; drain. Meanwhile, melt butter in a large skillet over medium heat. Stir in lemon juice and sauté mushrooms until tender. Stir in flour, salt and cayenne pepper. Gradually stir in milk. Cook until slightly thickened; stir in parsley. Spread half the mushroom mixture in a lightly greased 13"x9" baking pan. Alternate layers of noodles and ricotta, ending with ricotta. Top with remaining mushroom mixture. Sprinkle with Parmesan cheese. Bake, covered, at 350 degrees for 45 minutes. Let stand 15 minutes before serving. Makes 10 servings.

White Lasagna

Very Veggie Lasagna

Very Veggie Lasagna
Tina Nanney, Chandler, AZ

3 zucchini, sliced

8-oz. can mushrooms, drained and chopped

1 onion, chopped

4 cloves garlic, minced

3 T. olive oil

2 15-oz. containers ricotta cheese

1/4 c. grated Parmesan cheese

2 eggs

1 T. Italian seasoning

1/4 t. garlic salt

1/4 t. pepper

28-oz. jar spaghetti sauce, divided

16-oz. pkg. lasagna noodles, cooked

28-oz. can crushed tomatoes, divided

16-oz. pkg. shredded mozzarella cheese, divided

2 T. dried parsley

Sauté first 4 ingredients in olive oil for 5 minutes; set aside. In a medium bowl, combine ricotta cheese, Parmesan cheese, eggs and seasonings. In an ungreased 13"x9" baking pan, place one cup spaghetti sauce, then a layer of lasagna noodles. Spread half the sautéed vegetables on top of lasagna. Top with half the ricotta mixture. Top with next layer of lasagna and one cup tomatoes. Place remaining vegetables and ricotta mixture on top; sprinkle with one cup mozzarella cheese. Arrange remaining lasagna noodles and spread remaining sauce and tomatoes over lasagna. Sprinkle with remaining mozzarella cheese and top with parsley. Cover with aluminum foil and bake at 375 degrees for one hour. Uncover; bake an additional 5 minutes. Turn off oven and leave in for 20 minutes. Serves 12.

Oh-So-Hot Banana Peppers

Jean Cerutti, Kittanning, PA

18 hot banana peppers

2 6-oz. pkgs. pork-flavored stuffing mix, prepared

2 lbs. ground hot pork sausage, browned and drained

1 onion, chopped

1 zucchini, chopped

2 eggs, beaten

1/2 c. brown sugar, packed

16-oz. pkg. shredded Cheddar cheese

Slice peppers down center of one side lengthwise to open up; run under water, removing seeds. Combine prepared stuffing and sausage in a large bowl; add onion and zucchini. Stir in eggs and brown sugar; mix well. Spoon into peppers; arrange peppers in a lightly greased 13"x9" baking pan. Bake, uncovered, at 350 degrees for 1-1/2 hours. Sprinkle with cheese; bake for an additional 10 minutes, or until cheese is melted. Makes 12 servings.

Sour Cream-Chicken Enchiladas

Kim Turechek, Oklahoma City, OK

2 10-3/4 oz. cans cream of chicken soup

4-oz. can diced green chiles, drained

1/2 c. milk

1/2 t. ground cumin

1 c. sour cream

2 c. cooked chicken, cubed

3-oz. pkg. cream cheese, softened

1/4 c. onion, chopped

12 10-inch flour tortillas

1 c. Monterey Jack cheese, shredded

Combine the first 5 ingredients in a blender; blend until smooth. Set aside. Mix chicken, cream cheese and onion together; spread one to 2 tablespoons chicken mixture onto each tortilla. Roll up; place seam-side down in an ungreased 13"x9" baking pan. Top with sour cream mixture; sprinkle with cheese. Cover; bake at 350 degrees for 30 minutes. Uncover the last 5 minutes of baking. Makes 12 servings.

Creamy Taco Casserole

Cathy Wolf, Canton, TX

3 lbs. ground beef

1 onion, chopped

salt and pepper to taste

15-oz. can tomato sauce

4-1/2 oz. can chopped green chiles

2 10-oz. cans diced tomatoes with green chiles

1 c. hot pepper sauce

16 corn tortillas, torn into large pieces and divided

3 16-oz. pkgs. pasteurized processed cheese spread, sliced and divided

12-oz. can evaporated milk

Garnish: tortilla chips, additional hot pepper sauce

Brown ground beef with onion in a large skillet; sprinkle with salt and pepper. Drain; add tomato sauce, chiles, tomatoes with chiles and hot pepper sauce. Reduce heat to low and simmer for 20 minutes. Layer half of the tortillas, half of beef mixture and half of cheese in an ungreased 15"x10" jelly-roll pan sprayed with non-stick vegetable spray, pressing after each layer to pack. Repeat layers, reserving a little beef mixture to sprinkle over last cheese layer. Poke holes in the layers with a fork; pour evaporated milk over top. Allow milk to soak into casserole. Bake, uncovered, at 350 degrees for 40 to 45 minutes. Serve with chips and additional hot pepper sauce. Serves 10 to 12.

Quick tip

Casseroles are ideal for toting to neighborhood block parties. You'll enjoy catching up with friends while the kids race around playing games.

Oh-So-Hot Banana Peppers

Make-Ahead Potluck Potatoes

Make-Ahead Potluck Potatoes

Tracy Ruiz, Las Vegas, NV

12 russet potatoes, peeled, cubed and cooked
8-oz. pkg. cream cheese, softened
8-oz. container sour cream
1 t. onion powder
Optional: small amount milk or whipping cream
1/4 to 1/2 c. butter, melted
paprika to taste

Place warm potatoes in a large bowl; add cream cheese, sour cream and onion powder. Mash until fluffy, adding a small amount of milk or cream if desired. Spread in a greased 13"x9" baking pan. At this point, the potatoes can be baked immediately or covered and refrigerated for later. At baking time, drizzle with melted butter and sprinkle with a little paprika. Bake, uncovered, for one hour, or until heated through and golden. Makes 10 to 12 servings.

Fabulous Fruit & Nut Bake

April Jacobs, Loveland, CO

1 lb. ground pork sausage, browned and drained
1-1/2 c. sugar
1-1/2 c. brown sugar, packed
2 eggs, beaten
3 c. all-purpose flour
1 t. baking powder
1 t. ground ginger
1 t. pumpkin pie spice
1 t. baking soda
1 c. coffee, chilled
1 c. raisins
3 c. boiling water
1 c. chopped walnuts

Crumble sausage into small pieces in a large bowl; stir in sugars until mixture is well blended. Add eggs and beat well; set aside. In a separate bowl, sift together flour, baking powder, ginger and pumpkin pie spice; set aside. Stir baking soda into cold coffee. Add flour mixture and coffee alternately to sausage mixture, beating well after each addition. Combine raisins and water in a bowl; set aside for 5 to 10 minutes. Drain well; fold raisins and walnuts into cake batter. Turn batter into a well-greased Bundt® cake pan. Bake at 350 degrees for 1-1/2 hours, or until cake tests done. Cool in pan 15 minutes before turning out onto a serving platter. Serves 12.

Fabulous Fruit & Nut Bake

Quick tip

If you're adding more than one baking pan to the oven, remember to stagger them on the racks. Placing one pan directly over another won't allow the food to cook evenly in either pan.

Country Veggie Bake

Country Veggie Bake
Pat Griedl, Appleton, WI

1 to 2 T. olive oil
2 carrots, peeled, halved lengthwise and sliced
2 onions, chopped
1 to 2 cloves garlic, chopped
1 c. mushrooms, quartered
15-oz. can black beans, drained and rinsed
14-oz. can vegetable or chicken broth
1 c. frozen corn
1/2 c. pearled barley, uncooked
1/4 c. bulghur wheat, uncooked
1/3 c. fresh parsley, snipped
dried thyme to taste
1/2 to 1 c. shredded Cheddar cheese

Heat oil in a large skillet over medium heat. Sauté carrots and onions until carrots are tender. Stir in garlic and mushrooms; sauté 3 minutes. Combine mixture with remaining ingredients except cheese. Spoon into a greased 2-quart casserole dish. Bake, covered, at 350 degrees for one hour, stirring once halfway through baking time. Top with cheese. Cover and let stand 5 minutes, or until cheese melts. Makes 6 servings.

Curried Rice
Dorothy Jackson, Weddington, NC

1 lb. ground beef
1 c. long-cooking rice, uncooked
1 T. Worcestershire sauce
2 10-1/2 oz. cans beef
broth
2 t. curry powder
1 onion, chopped

In a large skillet, brown ground beef; drain. In a 13"x9" baking pan, combine all ingredients. Cover with aluminum foil and bake at 350 degrees for one hour. Makes 4 to 6 servings.

Quick tip
Small pears, apples and Jack-be-Little pumpkins make the sweetest placecards. Simply punch tags with holes, slip a ribbon though each and tie to the stem.

Curried Rice

Blue-Ribbon Summer Squash

Blue-Ribbon Summer Squash
Jamie Mills, Springfield, KY

8-1/2 oz. pkg. cornbread mix
4-1/2 c. yellow squash, sliced
4-1/2 c. zucchini, sliced
3/4 c. butter
1-1/2 c. onion, chopped
1 T. chicken soup base
1 t. garlic, minced
1/4 t. dried thyme
1 t. salt
1/2 t. pepper
2 c. shredded sharp Cheddar cheese

Prepare and bake cornbread mix according to package directions. Meanwhile, place squash and zucchini in a large Dutch oven; add just enough water to cover. Cook over medium heat just until tender. Drain squash in a colander, reserving one cup cooking liquid. In the same Dutch oven, melt butter over medium heat. Sauté onion until it turns clear; remove from heat. Add soup base, garlic and seasonings; stir until blended. Add drained squash and cheese; stir. Crumble cornbread into squash mixture; add reserved liquid and mix well. Spoon into a greased 13"x9" baking pan; cover with aluminum foil. Bake at 350 degrees for 50 to 60 minutes, uncovering for the last 20 minutes of baking time. Serves 8 to 10.

Swiss-Onion Casserole
Dolores McCurry, Pueblo, CO

6 onions, sliced
1/2 c. plus 3 T. butter, softened and divided
10-oz. pkg. shredded Swiss cheese
10-3/4 oz. can cream of mushroom with roasted garlic soup
1/2 c. milk
1 t. soy sauce
pepper to taste
12 to 15 slices baguette bread, sliced 1/2-inch thick

In a skillet over medium heat, sauté onions in 2 to 3 tablespoons butter until tender. Spread in a lightly greased 13"x9" baking pan. Cover with cheese; set aside. In a saucepan over medium heat, stir together soup, milk, soy sauce and pepper. Heat until bubbly; spoon over cheese. Spread remaining butter over both sides of bread. Arrange bread on top of casserole. Bake, uncovered, at 350 degrees for 30 minutes. Serves 10.

Good Morning Sausage Casserole
Beth Bundy, Long Prairie, MN

8-oz. tube refrigerated crescent rolls
1 lb. ground pork breakfast sausage, browned and drained
6 eggs, beaten
1/4 c. milk
salt and pepper to taste
2 c. shredded Cheddar cheese

Unroll crescent rolls into the bottom of a greased 13"x9" baking pan. Spoon browned sausage over rolls. Beat together eggs, milk, salt and pepper; pour over sausage. Sprinkle cheese on top. Bake, uncovered, at 350 degrees for 25 to 30 minutes. Makes 15 servings.

Quick tip
When topping a casserole with bread crumbs, potato chips or cereal, place in a plastic zipping bag and seal. Roll with a heavy rolling pin until the crumbs are crushed...clean-up is a breeze!

Pizzeria Sausage Supper

Kay Jones, Cleburne, TX

1 lb. ground pork sausage

1/2 c. onion, chopped

1/4 c. green pepper, chopped

2 T. all-purpose flour

16-oz. can diced tomatoes

4-oz. can mushroom stems & pieces, drained

1 t. fresh oregano, chopped

1/2 t. fresh basil, chopped

1/4 t. garlic powder

1/8 t. pepper

Optional: 4-oz. pkg. sliced pepperoni

10-oz. tube refrigerated biscuits, quartered

2 c. shredded mozzarella cheese

Optional: grated Parmesan cheese

In a large ovenproof skillet over medium heat, brown sausage, onion and pepper. Drain; sprinkle with flour. Add undrained tomatoes, mushrooms and seasonings; mix well. Simmer until hot and bubbly, stirring until slightly thickened. Add pepperoni, if desired. Arrange biscuit quarters over mixture in skillet. Sprinkle biscuit layer with mozzarella cheese. Bake, uncovered, at 400 degrees for 12 to 16 minutes, until biscuits are golden. Garnish with Parmesan, if desired. Makes about 10 servings.

Quick tip

Do the unexpected! Brand new terra cotta saucers lined with tea towels make fun platters for serving bread, buns or biscuits.

Mary's Macaroni & Cheese

Mary Casasanta, Tracy, CA

16-oz. pkg. elbow macaroni, cooked

1/2 c. butter, diced

16-oz. container sharp Cheddar cheese spread

2 c. shredded Colby Jack cheese

2 eggs, beaten

12-oz. can evaporated milk

1 c. shredded Cheddar cheese

1 c. panko bread crumbs or plain dry bread crumbs

In a large bowl, mix together all ingredients except Cheddar cheese and bread crumbs. Pour into a greased 13"x9" baking pan. Top with Cheddar cheese and bread crumbs. Bake, uncovered, at 350 degrees for 30 minutes, until bubbly and golden. Makes 10 servings.

Tailgaters' Penne Pasta

Debi King, Reisterstown, MD

1-1/2 lbs. ground beef

1 lb. hot pork sausage, sliced 1/2-inch thick

1 c. onion, chopped

2 t. dried oregano

16-oz. pkg. mini penne pasta, uncooked

2 10-3/4 oz. cans Cheddar cheese soup

2 10-3/4 oz. cans tomato soup

2 c. water

4 slices Cheddar cheese, sliced diagonally

In a large, deep oven-safe skillet over medium heat, brown beef, sausage, onion and oregano. Break up meat with a spatula as it cooks; drain. Meanwhile, cook pasta according to package directions; drain. Add pasta, soups and water to mixture in skillet; stir well. Cover skillet and place in a cold oven. Turn to 400 degrees and bake for 40 minutes, or until hot. Remove from oven; arrange cheese slices on top. Return to oven and bake 3 to 4 additional minutes, until cheese melts. Serves 10.

Pizzeria Sausage Supper

Go-Withs

Need a tasty dish to go with your chicken & spaghetti casserole? Maple-glazed carrots might be just the ticket. From fresh summer salads to swirled coffee cake and strudel, these fun and mouthwatering dishes can help make your casserole a meal!

Fresh Kale Salad

Fresh Kale Salad

Carol Werner, Brooklyn Park, MN

3 T. honey
1/2 c. olive or canola oil
juice of 1 lemon
pepper to taste
1 bunch fresh kale, torn
  and stems removed

1/2 c. raisins or dried
  cranberries
1/4 c. sunflower kernels

In a large bowl, combine honey, oil, lemon juice and pepper. Whisk until blended. Add kale and toss to coat; let stand about 5 minutes. Sprinkle with raisins or cranberries and sunflower seeds; toss again. Serves 6.

Cool Summer Salad

Chris Lercel, Covina, CA

1 cucumber, sliced
2 to 3 tomatoes, diced
1/4 red onion, thinly sliced

1 avocado, halved, pitted
  and cubed
1/2 c. Italian salad dressing

Combine all vegetables in a bowl. Drizzle salad dressing over top. Refrigerate, covered, for at least one hour. Toss gently before serving. Serves 4 to 6.

Cool Summer Salad

Quick tip

Until they're ready for your best recipe, tuck sprigs of fresh herbs into water-filled Mason jars or votive holders for a few days. Not only will they stay fresh longer, they'll look so lovely!

Peppery Olive Focaccia

Eleanor Dionne, Beverly, MA

2 1-lb. loaves frozen bread
  dough, thawed
2 T. olive oil
2 cloves garlic, minced
1/3 c. black or green olives,
  chopped
1/8 to 1/4 t. red pepper
  flakes

1 t. fresh rosemary,
  minced, or 1/2 t. dried
  rosemary
1/2 c. shredded Parmesan
  cheese

Lightly grease a 15"x10" jelly-roll pan. Pat and stretch dough to fit into pan. Drizzle with olive oil. Sprinkle with remaining ingredients. Allow to rise at room temperature for one hour. Bake at 375 degrees for 12 to 14 minutes, until golden. Cut into squares. Serves 8 to 12.

Go-Withs

Cow-Country Beans
Debra Crisp, Grants Pass, OR

3 c. dried red beans
1 lb. cooked ham, cubed
1 onion, sliced
1 c. celery, diced
8-oz. can tomato sauce
2 T. bacon bits

2 T. chili powder
1 T. brown sugar, packed
2 t. garlic powder
1/2 t. smoke-flavored
  cooking sauce
1/2 t. salt

Cover dried beans with water in a bowl; soak overnight. Drain beans; combine with remaining ingredients in a slow cooker. Cover and cook on high setting for 8 to 10 hours. Makes 8 to 10 servings.

Cow-Country Beans

Maple-Glazed Carrots
Andrea Heyart, Aubrey, TX

4-1/2 c. water
4 lbs. carrots, peeled and
  sliced
10 T. butter, divided
6 T. brown sugar, packed
  and divided

1-1/2 t. salt
6 T. maple syrup
Garnish: snipped fresh
  chives

Bring water to a boil in a large saucepan over medium-high heat. Add carrots, 4 tablespoons butter, 3 tablespoons brown sugar and salt. Reduce heat to medium-low. Cover and simmer just until carrots are tender when pierced with a fork, about 10 minutes. Drain and set aside. Melt remaining butter in a large skillet over medium-high heat. Add maple syrup and remaining brown sugar; cook and stir until sugar has dissolved. Reduce heat to medium-low. Add carrots to syrup mixture and toss gently. Cook for 5 minutes, or until carrots are evenly coated and mixture is bubbly. Sprinkle with chives just before serving. Serves 10.

Quick tip
Mint is an easy herb to grow and nice in so many recipes. Planted in a garden though, it tends to spread quickly. To keep mint only where you want it, it's best to tuck plants into containers. Keep a variety by the kitchen door...peppermint, spearmint and applemint.

Maple-Glazed Carrots

Quick & Easy Lemon Bars

Quick & Easy Lemon Bars
Lynda McCormick, Burkburnett, TX

16-oz. pkg. angel food cake
  mix
22-oz. can lemon pie filling

Optional: chopped pecans,
  sweetened flaked
  coconut

Combine dry cake mix and pie filling in a large bowl; mix well. Spread in a greased 15"x10" jelly-roll pan; top with pecans or coconut, if desired. Bake at 350 degrees for 30 minutes. Let cool; cut into bars. Makes 2-1/2 dozen.

Sausage Stars
Tina Butler, Royse City, TX

1 lb. ground pork sausage
1-oz. pkg. ranch salad
  dressing mix
8-oz. pkg. shredded
  Mexican-blend cheese

Optional: 1/2 c. green or
  red pepper, chopped
12-oz. pkg. wonton
  wrappers or egg roll
  wrappers

Brown sausage in a skillet over medium-high heat; drain and set aside. Prepare salad dressing mix according to package directions. Combine cooled sausage, dressing, cheese and pepper, if using; chill for 30 minutes. Place one wonton wrapper into each cup of a lightly greased muffin tin. Push down gently to form a little shell-like cup. Bake 5 to 7 minutes, just until lightly golden. Watch carefully; do not allow cups to turn brown. Remove from oven; let cool. Fill each cup with about 2 tablespoons of sausage mixture. Bake 5 to 7 minutes longer, until cheese melts. Cool before serving. Makes about 4 dozen.

Sweet Potato Toss
Janet Monnett, Cloverdale, IN

2 sweet potatoes, peeled
  and sliced
4 potatoes, peeled and
  sliced

1/2 to 1 T. onion powder
1/8 t. sugar
salt to taste

Into a skillet over medium-high heat, add oil to 1/2-inch depth. Combine all potato slices in a bowl; toss with seasonings. Add potatoes to hot oil in skillet. Cover and cook, turning as needed. Reduce heat to medium when potatoes begin to soften. Uncover for the last 3 to 4 minutes of cooking to crisp up potatoes. Serves 4 to 6.

Quick tip
To keep just-cut fruit slices looking fresh, dip them into lemon-lime soda before serving.

Blue Goose Pie
Jean Manahan, Waynesboro, PA

2 c. fresh gooseberries
2-1/2 c. fresh blueberries
3/4 c. sugar
1/4 t. salt
1/2 t. cinnamon
1/4 c. cornstarch
2 9-inch pie crusts
1 T. butter, sliced

In a bowl, mix together berries, sugar, salt, cinnamon and cornstarch; toss to coat berries well. Line a 9" pie plate with one pie crust. Pour berry mixture into crust; dot with butter. Cover with top crust; seal and vent crust. Bake pie at 450 degrees for 50 minutes, or until crust is golden and filling is bubbly. Serves 8

Blue Pan Cranberry Cake
Karen Urfer, New Philadelphia, OH

1 c. fresh cranberries
3/4 c. sugar, divided
1/4 c. chopped walnuts
1 egg
1/2 c. all-purpose flour
6 T. butter, melted
Garnish: whipped cream
   or ice cream

Spread cranberries in a greased 9" pie plate. Sprinkle cranberries with 1/4 cup sugar and walnuts; set aside. In a bowl, beat together egg and remaining sugar. Add flour and melted butter; beat well and pour over cranberries. Bake at 325 degrees for 40 to 45 minutes, until golden on top. Garnish as desired. Serves 8.

Champagne Fruit Salad
Elizabeth Burkhalter, Oshkosh, WI

8-oz. pkg. cream cheese,
   softened
3/4 c. sugar
10-oz. pkg. frozen sliced
   strawberries, thawed and
   drained
2 bananas, sliced
8-oz. can crushed
   pineapple, drained
1 c. chopped pecans
1 c. sweetened flaked
   coconut
10-oz. container frozen
   whipped topping, thawed

In a large bowl, blend together cream cheese and sugar with an electric mixer on medium speed. Stir in remaining ingredients by hand. Spread in a 3-quart baking pan. Cover and freeze until firm, 3 to 4 hours. Remove from freezer a few minutes before serving time; cut into squares. Serve in champagne glasses, if desired. Serves 12.

Blue Pan Cranberry Cake

Blue Goose Pie

Angel Strudel

Angel Strudel

Jo Baker, Litchfield, IL

1 c. butter
2 c. all-purpose flour
3 egg yolks
2 T. vinegar
1/4 c. water
1 c. walnuts, ground
1 c. maraschino cherries, chopped
18-1/4 oz. pkg. angel food cake mix

In a large bowl, cut butter into flour until mixture resembles coarse crumbs; set aside. In a separate bowl, whisk together egg yolks, vinegar and water; add to butter mixture and mix well. Divide dough into 4 portions; cover and refrigerate 8 hours to overnight. When ready to prepare strudel, roll out one portion of dough into a very thin rectangle. In a bowl, combine walnuts, cherries and dry cake mix; divide into 4 equal portions. Spread one portion of the filling on rolled dough. Roll up, starting at one short edge. Repeat with remaining 3 portions of dough and filling. Place each on an ungreased baking sheet. Bake each strudel at 325 degrees for 25 minutes. Slice to serve. Makes 4 strudels; each serves 8 to 10.

Country Sausage & Apples

Country Sausage & Apples

Donna Maltman, Toledo, OH

1-lb. pkg. smoked pork sausage, sliced into 1-inch pieces
3 Granny Smith apples, cored and diced
1 c. brown sugar, packed
1/4 to 1/2 c. water

Place sausage in a slow cooker; top with apples. Sprinkle with brown sugar and drizzle water over all. Stir gently; cover and cook on high setting for 1-1/2 to 2 hours, until apples are tender. Makes 4 servings.

Quick tip

Gardens turn up the best pizza toppers...try something new like chopped spinach, green onions, chives, cilantro, asparagus, sliced roma tomatoes or shredded carrots.

Easy Bacon Frittata
Beth Bundy, Long Prairie, MN

3 T. oil
2 c. frozen shredded
  hashbrowns
7 eggs, beaten
2 T. milk

12 slices bacon, crisply
  cooked and crumbled
3/4 c. shredded Cheddar
  cheese

Heat oil in a large skillet over medium heat. Add hashbrowns and cook for 10 to 15 minutes, stirring often, until golden. In a bowl, whisk together eggs and milk. Pour egg mixture over hashbrowns in skillet; sprinkle with bacon. Cover and reduce heat to low. Cook for 10 minutes, or until eggs are set. Sprinkle with cheese; remove from heat, cover, and let stand about 5 minutes, until cheese is melted. Cut into wedges to serve. Makes 6 servings.

Cream Cheesy Mexican Corn
Anne Welborn, Fort Wayne, IN

2 15-oz. cans corn,
  drained
1/2 green pepper, diced

1/2 red pepper, diced
8-oz. pkg. cream cheese,
  cubed

Combine all ingredients in a saucepan over medium-low heat. Cook, stirring occasionally, until cream cheese melts and peppers are cooked through. Serves 6.

Easy Bacon Frittata

Spinach Quiche
Glenda Tolbert, Moore, SC

12-oz. pkg. frozen spinach
  soufflé, thawed
2 eggs, beaten
3 T. milk
2 t. onion, chopped
3/4 c. Italian ground pork
  sausage, browned and
  drained

1/2 c. sliced mushrooms
3/4 c. shredded Swiss
  cheese
9-inch pie crust, baked

In a bowl, mix together all ingredients except crust; pour into crust. Bake at 400 degrees for 30 to 45 minutes, until golden and center is set. Cut into wedges. Serves 6.

Quick tip
I have never had so many good ideas day after day as when I worked in the garden.
-John Erskine

Spinach Quiche

Swirled Coffee Cake

Swirled Coffee Cake

Carol Doiron, North Berwick, ME

18-1/4 oz. pkg. yellow cake mix
5-1/4 oz. pkg. instant pistachio pudding mix
4 eggs, beaten
1 t. vanilla extract
1 c. water
1/2 c. oil
1/2 c. sugar
2 t. cinnamon
1/2 c. chopped walnuts

Combine dry cake mix and dry pudding mix in a large bowl; blend in eggs, vanilla, water and oil. Pour half the batter into a greased Bundt® pan; set aside. Mix together sugar, cinnamon and walnuts in a small bowl; sprinkle half over batter in pan. Swirl in with a knife; add remaining batter. Swirl in remaining sugar mixture. Bake at 350 degrees for 50 minutes, or until cake tests done with a toothpick. Cool in pan and remove to a serving platter. Makes 12 to 15 servings.

Impossibly Easy BLT Pie

Athena Colegrove, Big Springs, TX

12 slices bacon, crisply cooked and crumbled
1 c. shredded Swiss cheese
1/2 c. biscuit baking mix
1/3 c. plus 2 T. mayonnaise, divided
3/4 c. milk
1/8 t. pepper
2 eggs, beaten
1 c. shredded lettuce
6 thin slices tomato

Layer bacon and cheese in a lightly greased 9" pie plate. In a bowl, whisk together baking mix, 1/3 cup mayonnaise, milk, pepper and eggs until blended. Pour over cheese. Bake at 350 degrees for 25 to 30 minutes, until top is golden and a knife inserted in center comes out clean. Let stand 5 minutes. Spread remaining mayonnaise over pie. Sprinkle with lettuce; arrange tomato slices over lettuce. Serves 6.

Tart Apple Salad

Leona Krivda, Belle Vernon, PA

6 tart crisp apples, peeled, cored and chopped
1-1/2 c. red grapes, halved and seeded
1 c. celery, finely chopped
1/2 c. chopped walnuts
1/4 c. sugar
1 T. mayonnaise-style salad dressing
1/2 pt. whipping cream, whipped
1/4 c. sweetened dried cranberries

Toss together apples, grapes, celery and walnuts in a large serving bowl; sprinkle with sugar. Stir in salad dressing; mix well. Cover and chill until serving time. Fold in whipped cream and cranberries just before serving. Serves 10 to 12.

Impossibly Easy BLT Pie

Go-Withs

Sweet Apple Butter Muffins
The Inn At Shadow Lawn, Middletown, RI

1-3/4 c. all-purpose flour
1/3 c. plus 2 T. sugar, divided
2 t. baking powder
1/2 t. cinnamon
1/4 t. nutmeg
1/4 t. salt
1 egg, beaten
3/4 c. milk
1/4 c. oil
1 t. vanilla extract
1/3 c. apple butter
1/3 c. chopped pecans

Combine flour, 1/3 cup sugar, baking powder, spices and salt in a large bowl; set aside. In a separate bowl, blend egg, milk, oil and vanilla together; stir into flour mixture. Spoon one tablespoon batter into each of 12 paper-lined muffin cups; top with one teaspoon apple butter. Fill muffin cups 2/3 full using remaining batter; set aside. Toss pecans with remaining sugar; sprinkle evenly over muffins. Bake at 400 degrees until a toothpick inserted in the center tests clean, about 20 minutes. Makes one dozen.

Autumn Acorn Squash
Jenny Sarbacker, Madison, WI

2 acorn squash, halved and seeded
2 apples, peeled, cored and chopped
3 T. brown sugar, packed
3 T. chopped pecans
1 t. all-purpose flour
1/4 t. cinnamon
2 T. butter, softened

Place acorn squash halves cut-side down in a greased 3-quart casserole dish. Bake at 350 degrees for 30 minutes. Combine remaining ingredients. Turn squash over and fill with apple mixture. Bake, uncovered, for another 15 to 30 minutes, until squash is soft when pierced with a fork. Serve squash halves as is or scoop contents into a serving bowl. Serves 4.

String Beans & Corn Casserole
Donna Clement, Picayune, MS

2 14-1/2 oz. cans French-cut green beans, drained
2 15-oz. cans shoepeg corn, drained
1/4 c. onion, chopped
1/4 c. celery, chopped
8-oz. container sour cream
10-3/4 oz. can cream of celery soup
4-1/2 oz. pkg. cheese crackers, crushed
1/4 c. margarine, melted
Garnish: slivered almonds

In a bowl, mix vegetables, sour cream and soup. Place in a lightly greased 3-quart baking pan. Mix crushed crackers and melted margarine; sprinkle over casserole, followed by almonds. Bake, uncovered, at 375 degrees for 30 minutes, or until hot and bubbly. Makes 8 to 12 servings.

Quick tip
Once summertime herbs have dried, store them in jars with biscuit-topper lids...how clever! Search flea markets for biscuit cutters, then purchase new jars whose lids will fit inside the cutters. Secure new lids inside the cutters with metal adhesive and let dry.

Sweet Apple Butter Muffins

Best-Ever Spinach Salad

Best-Ever Spinach Salad
Pamela Forrester, Pontoon Beach, IL

1 bunch fresh spinach, torn
6 eggs, hard-boiled, peeled and sliced
1 lb. bacon, crisply cooked and crumbled
1/2 c. olive oil
1/4 c. sugar
2 T. cider vinegar
1/2 t. salt
1/4 t. dry mustard
Optional: 1 T. dried, minced onion

In a large bowl, combine spinach, eggs and bacon. In a separate bowl, whisk together remaining ingredients. Before serving, drizzle dressing over spinach mixture and toss lightly to coat. Serves 8 to 10.

Sunflower Strawberry Salad
Sister Toni Spencer, Watertown, SD

2 c. strawberries, hulled and sliced
1 apple, cored and diced
1 c. seedless green grapes, halved
1/2 c. celery, thinly sliced
1/4 c. raisins
1/2 c. strawberry yogurt
2 T. sunflower kernels
Optional: lettuce leaves

In a large bowl, combine fruit, celery and raisins. Stir in yogurt. Cover and chill one hour. Sprinkle with sunflower kernels just before serving. Spoon over lettuce leaves, if desired. Makes 6 servings.

Sunflower Strawberry Salad

Simmered Autumn Applesauce
Jennifer Levy, Warners, NY

8 apples, several different varieties, peeled, cored and cubed
1 c. water
1/2 c. brown sugar, packed
1 t. cinnamon
1/2 t. pumpkin pie spice

Add all ingredients to a slow cooker; stir. Cover and cook on low setting for 6 to 8 hours. Mash apples with the back of a spoon; stir again. Let cool slightly before serving. Makes 6 servings.

Quick tip
Snap up roomy gallon-size Mason jars when you spot them...just right for holding lots of iced tea or lemonade.

Go-Withs

Cabbage-Tomato Slaw
Tamara Parlor, Hazelhurst, GA

1 head cabbage, chopped
1 sweet onion, chopped
2 tomatoes, diced
1/2 c. mayonnaise
salt and pepper to taste

Combine all ingredients in a large salad bowl. Toss to mix; cover and refrigerate until serving time. Toss again before serving. Makes 6 to 8 servings.

Peachy-Keen Sweet Taters
Cathi Carpenter, Marietta, GA

2-1/4 c. sweet potatoes, peeled and cubed
21-oz. can peach pie filling
2 T. butter, melted
1 t. fresh ginger, peeled and grated, or 1 t. ground ginger
1/4 t. salt
2 T. brown sugar, packed
1/8 t. cinnamon
1/2 c. pecans, coarsely chopped

Place sweet potatoes in a 4-quart slow cooker sprayed with non-stick vegetable spray. Add pie filling, butter, ginger and salt; mix well to coat. Cover and cook on high setting for 2-1/2 to 3 hours. In a small saucepan over medium-low heat, combine remaining ingredients. Cook until glazed and bubbly, stirring frequently. Spoon pecans onto an aluminum foil-lined baking sheet to cool. Just before serving, gently stir potatoes; sprinkle with pecans. Serves 6.

Cabbage-Tomato Slaw

Pea Salad
Dee Faulding, Santa Barbara, CA

1 c. elbow macaroni, cooked
3 slices bacon, crisply cooked and crumbled
1/2 c. green onion, chopped
2 c. frozen baby peas, thawed
1 c. mayonnaise
1/2 c. shredded Cheddar cheese

In a bowl, combine macaroni, bacon, green onions and peas. Stir in mayonnaise; cover and refrigerate for at least 2 hours. Sprinkle with cheese just before serving. Serves 4 to 6.

Pea Salad

Apple-Walnut Chicken Salad

Apple-Walnut Chicken Salad

Becky Butler, Keller, TX

6 c. mixed field greens or baby greens

2 c. deli roast chicken, shredded

1/3 c. crumbled blue cheese

1/4 c. chopped walnuts, toasted

1 Fuji or Gala apple, cored and chopped

In a large salad bowl, toss together all ingredients. Drizzle Balsamic Apple Vinaigrette over salad, tossing gently to coat. Serve immediately. Makes 6 servings.

Balsamic Apple Vinaigrette:

2 T. frozen apple juice concentrate

1 T. cider vinegar

1 T. white balsamic vinegar

1 t. Dijon mustard

1/4 t. garlic powder

1/3 c. olive oil

Whisk together all ingredients in a small bowl.

Fusilli Garden Salad

Sharon Tillman, Hampton, VA

16-oz. pkg. fusilli pasta, uncooked and divided

1 yellow squash, halved lengthwise and sliced

1 c. cherry tomatoes

1 c. snow pea pods

1 c. green olives with pimentos

4 green onions, thinly sliced

1 c. Cheddar cheese, diced

1 c. sliced almonds, toasted

8-oz. bottle Italian salad dressing

1 c. black olives

Divide pasta in half, reserving the remainder for a future use. Cook remaining pasta according to package directions; drain and rinse with cold water. In a large bowl, combine cooked pasta and remaining ingredients except salad dressing. Add desired amount of salad dressing; toss gently to coat. Cover and chill at least 2 hours before serving. Serves 12.

Honey-Mustard Sweet Potatoes

Tara Horton, Delaware, OH

1 T. margarine

1/2 c. onion, thinly sliced

3 sweet potatoes, peeled and cut into 1-inch cubes

1 c. chicken broth

1 T. Dijon mustard

1 T. honey

1/4 t. pepper

Melt margarine in a saucepan over medium heat. Sauté onion and sweet potatoes for 5 minutes. Stir in remaining ingredients; bring to a boil. Reduce heat; cover and simmer for 20 minutes, or until potatoes are tender. Remove from heat; whip with an electric mixer on medium speed until smooth. Serves 4.

Quick tip

Add a burst of flavor to a glass of water...toss in fresh berries, melon or apple slices.

Wild Blueberry Gingerbread

Gail Hageman, Albion, ME

2-1/2 c. all-purpose flour	1/2 c. molasses
1 c. sugar	2 eggs, beaten
1/2 t. ground cloves	1/2 c. oil
1/2 t. cinnamon	1 c. hot tea
1/2 t. ground ginger	1 c. fresh blueberries
1 t. salt	Garnish: whipped cream
1 t. baking soda	

In a large bowl, mix together flour, sugar, spices and baking soda. Stir in molasses, eggs, oil and tea. Carefully fold in blueberries. Spoon batter into a greased and floured 13"x9" baking pan. Bake at 350 degrees for about 35 minutes, until a toothpick inserted in the center tests clean. Cool; cut into squares and top with a dollop of whipped cream. Makes 13 to 15 servings.

Wild Blueberry Gingerbread

Cinnamon Gingersnaps

Lisa Ashton, Aston, PA

3/4 c. butter, softened	2 t. baking soda
1 c. brown sugar, packed	1/2 t. salt
1 egg, beaten	2 t. cinnamon
1/4 c. molasses	1 t. ground ginger
2-1/4 c. all-purpose flour	1/2 to 1 c. sugar

Blend together butter and brown sugar in a large bowl. Mix in egg and molasses; set aside. In a separate bowl, combine flour, baking soda, salt, cinnamon and ginger. Gradually add flour mixture to butter mixture; mix well. Roll dough into one-inch balls; roll in sugar. Arrange 2 inches apart on ungreased baking sheets. Bake at 350 degrees for 10 to 12 minutes, until cookies are set and tops are cracked. Remove to wire racks; cool completely. Makes 4 dozen.

Corn Mazatlán

Tracee Cummins, Amarillo, TX

16-oz. can corn, drained and 1/4 cup liquid reserved	1/4 c. green onions, chopped
8-oz. pkg. cream cheese, softened	2 4-oz. cans chopped green chiles
16-oz. can shoepeg corn, drained	1 t. ground cumin
1/4 c. green pepper, chopped	

In a saucepan over low heat, combine reserved corn liquid and cream cheese. Cook and stir until smooth. Stir in remaining ingredients and heat through. Serves 8 to 10.

Cinnamon Gingersnaps

Hucklebucks

Shannon Ellis, Mount Vernon, WA

3/4 c. shortening
2 eggs, beaten
3/4 c. baking cocoa
1-1/2 c. sugar
3 t. vanilla extract, divided
1-1/2 c. all-purpose flour
1 T. baking powder

3/4 t. plus 1/8 t. salt, divided
1-1/2 c. plus 1 T. milk, divided
3/4 c. butter, softened
2 c. powdered sugar
1 c. marshmallow creme

In a large bowl, beat together shortening, eggs, cocoa, sugar and 1-1/2 teaspoons vanilla. In a separate bowl, sift together flour, baking powder and 3/4 teaspoon salt. Add 1-1/2 cups milk to cocoa mixture, alternating with dry ingredients. Mix well after each addition until batter is smooth. Drop by tablespoonfuls onto ungreased baking sheets. Bake at 400 degrees for 7 to 8 minutes; cool. Blend together remaining vanilla, salt, milk and other ingredients; spread on one side of a cookie and top with a second cookie. Repeat with remaining cookies. Makes 2 dozen.

Hucklebucks

Root Beer Cake

Root Beer Cake

Tish DeYoung, Wausau, WI

1 c. sugar	2 c. all-purpose flour
1/2 c. butter, softened	1 T. baking powder
1/2 t. vanilla extract	1 t. salt
2 eggs, beaten	2/3 c. root beer

Combine all ingredients in a large bowl. Blend with an electric mixer on low speed; beat for 3 minutes on medium speed. Pour into a greased and floured 8"x8" baking pan. Bake at 375 degrees for 30 to 35 minutes, until a toothpick tests clean. Spread Frosting over cooled cake. Serves 8 to 10.

Frosting:

1/4 c. butter	2 to 4 T. milk
1/8 t. salt	1/3 c. root beer, chilled
2 c. powdered sugar	

In a bowl, beat together all ingredients except root beer. Add root beer; beat to desired consistency.

Go-Withs

Zucchini Patties
Linda McGowan, Riverside, RI

1-1/2 c. zucchini, shredded and pressed dry
1 c. panko bread crumbs
2 T. onion, finely chopped
2 T. all-purpose flour
1 T. mayonnaise
1 t. seafood seasoning
2 eggs, beaten
oil for frying
Garnish: applesauce, sour cream or catsup

In a large bowl, combine zucchini, bread crumbs, onion, flour, mayonnaise and seasoning. Add eggs, stirring well to combine. Shape into 10 patties. Add enough oil in a large skillet to equal 1/2-inch depth; heat over medium heat until hot. Fry patties for one to 2 minutes per side, until golden. Drain on paper towels. Serve with sour cream, applesauce or catsup. Makes 10 servings.

Mom's Cucumber Gelatin Salad
Natasha Morris, Lamar, CO

3-oz. pkg. lime gelatin mix
1 t. salt
1 c. boiling water
2 T. vinegar
1 t. onion, grated
1/8 t. pepper
1 c. sour cream
1/2 c. mayonnaise
2 c. cucumbers, peeled and diced

Combine gelatin mix and salt with boiling water; stir until dissolved. Add vinegar, onion and pepper; cover and refrigerate about one hour, until very thick. Blend in sour cream and mayonnaise; fold in cucumbers. Return to refrigerator for 3 to 4 hours, until set. Serves 10.

Gingersnap Baked Beans
Nancy Elder, Lincoln, NE

4 slices bacon, crisply cooked and crumbled
2 16-oz. cans pork & beans
2 T. onion, chopped
1/4 c. brown sugar, packed
1/4 c. catsup
3/4 c. gingersnap cookies, crushed

In a large bowl, mix together all ingredients. Spoon into a greased 1-1/2 quart casserole dish. Bake, uncovered, at 375 degrees for 30 minutes, or until hot and bubbly. Serves 6 to 8.

Spicy Green Beans
Faye Saterfield, Monroe, LA

3 14-1/2 oz. cans French-cut green beans, drained
6 slices bacon, crisply cooked and crumbled, drippings reserved
Cajun seasoning to taste

In a skillet over medium heat, cook green beans in reserved drippings until heated through. Sprinkle with desired amount of seasoning; top with crumbled bacon. Serves 6.

Quick tip
Spooned over avocado halves, Santa Fe-style dressing is so yummy! Combine 2 tablespoons mayonnaise with 1/4 teaspoon garlic powder, 1/8 teaspoon red pepper flakes and 1/2 teaspoon cumin. Stir in some finely chopped fresh cilantro and chill 30 minutes.

Zucchini Patties

Mac & Cheese Cupcakes

Mac & Cheese Cupcakes

Shelley Turner, Boise, ID

8-oz. pkg. elbow macaroni, cooked

1 t. olive oil

1-1/2 c. milk

2 T. cornstarch

1 t. Dijon mustard

salt and pepper to taste

2 c. shredded sharp Cheddar cheese

1/2 c. seasoned dry bread crumbs

Toss macaroni with olive oil; set aside. In a medium saucepan, whisk milk and cornstarch until blended. Bring to a boil over medium heat, stirring often. Stir in mustard, salt and pepper. Reduce heat and simmer until thickened, stirring frequently. Add cheese and stir until melted; fold in macaroni. Grease 12 muffin cups with butter, coat with bread crumbs and shake off excess. Spoon in macaroni mixture. Bake at 350 degrees for 15 to 25 minutes, until golden. Makes one dozen.

Kids' Favorite Fruit Salad

Kids' Favorite Fruit Salad

Carrie Fostor, Baltic, OH

14-1/2 oz. can peach pie filling

1 c. pineapple, peeled and diced

1 c. seedless red grapes

2 bananas, sliced

11-oz. can mandarin oranges, drained

1 c. mini marshmallows

Mix all ingredients together in a large bowl and refrigerate until chilled. Serves 6 to 8.

Quick tip

Toasting pine nuts is so easy. Place them in a dry skillet over medium heat. Stir occasionally until lightly golden...about 3 minutes. Cool, then add to sandwiches or salads.

Easy Rice Pilaf

Robbi Buckles, Coldwater, MI

1/2 c. butter, melted

1-1/2 c. long-cooking rice, uncooked

10-1/2 oz. can beef consommé or beef broth

10-1/2 oz. can French onion soup

1 c. shredded Cheddar cheese

Combine all ingredients together except cheese. Pour into a greased 2-quart casserole dish with lid. Bake, covered, at 350 degrees for one hour. Remove from oven; sprinkle with cheese. Cover; let stand 3 to 5 minutes, until cheese has melted. Serves 6.

Chapter 7

Sweet Treat Desserts

Crisps, cobblers, cakes and pies...the warm-you-up desserts we all love. Whether you're craving a fruity cranberry-apple crisp or a decadent chocolate icebox cake, these simple-to-make, delicious desserts are the perfect ending to any meal.

Cherries Jubilee Crisp

Buttermilk Pear Cobbler

Trysha Mapley-Barron, Palmer, AK

3 lbs. Anjou or Bosc pears, peeled, cored and sliced
1/3 c. brown sugar, packed
1 T. all-purpose flour
1 T. lemon juice
1 t. cinnamon
1/4 t. nutmeg
1/4 t. mace

Combine all ingredients in a large bowl. Toss gently and spoon into a lightly greased 8"x8" baking pan. Drop biscuit topping by heaping tablespoonfuls onto pear mixture. Bake at 350 degrees for 45 minutes, or until bubbly and lightly golden. Serves 8.

Biscuit Topping:
1 c. all-purpose flour
1 T. baking powder
2 T. sugar
3 T. buttermilk
1/2 c. cold butter
3/4 c. milk

Mix together flour, baking powder, sugar and buttermilk. Cut in butter with a fork until mixture is crumbly; add milk and mix well.

Buttermilk Pear Cobbler

Quick tip

Don't toss that lemon or orange half after it's been juiced! Wrap it and store in the freezer, and it'll be ready to grate whenever a recipe calls for fresh citrus zest.

Cherries Jubilee Crisp

Jill Valentine, Jackson, TN

15-oz. can dark sweet cherries
2 T. orange liqueur or orange juice
2-1/2 t. cornstarch
1/4 c. quick-cooking oats, uncooked
6 T. all-purpose flour
1/4 c. brown sugar, packed
1/4 t. nutmeg
1/4 c. cold butter, diced
Optional: whipped cream, nutmeg

Combine undrained cherries, liqueur or juice and cornstarch in a saucepan. Cook and stir over medium heat about 2 minutes, until cornstarch dissolves and mixture thickens. Pour into a lightly greased one-quart casserole dish; let cool for 10 minutes. In a small bowl, stir together oats, flour, brown sugar and nutmeg. Add butter; mix with a fork until crumbly. Sprinkle oat mixture over cherry mixture. Bake at 375 degrees for about 20 minutes, until topping is golden. Serve warm, topped with whipped cream and a sprinkle of nutmeg, if desired. Serves 4.

Virginia Apple Pudding
Jeannie Wolf, Findlay, OH

2-1/4 c. apples, peeled,
  cored and sliced
1/2 c. butter, sliced
1 c. sugar
1 c. all-purpose flour
2 t. baking powder
1/4 t. salt
1/4 t. cinnamon
1 c. milk
Garnish: whipped cream,
  ice cream or lemon sauce

In a saucepan, cover apples with water. Cook over medium-high heat just until tender, about 5 minutes; drain well. Place butter in a 2-quart casserole dish; melt in oven at 375 degrees. In a bowl, stir together remaining ingredients except garnish; pour over butter in dish. Do not stir. Spoon apples into center of batter; do not stir. Bake at 375 degrees for about 40 minutes, until batter covers fruit and crust forms. Serve warm or cold; garnish as desired. Serves 4 to 6.

Virginia Apple Pudding

First-Prize Peach Cobbler
Debbie Desormeaux, Lafayette, LA

18-1/2 oz. pkg. yellow cake
  mix
29-oz. can sliced peaches
15-oz. can sliced peaches
1/2 c. half-and-half
1/2 c. sugar
1/2 c. butter, sliced
Garnish: whipped cream
  or vanilla ice cream

Add dry cake mix to a 3-quart casserole dish sprayed with non-stick vegetable spray. Make a well in the center of cake mix. Add undrained peaches and half-and-half; stir to blend and moisten. Sprinkle with sugar; dot with butter. Cover and refrigerate 8 hours to overnight to allow flavors to blend. Bake at 350 degrees for one hour, or until bubbly and golden. Serve warm or cold, garnished as desired. Makes 6 to 8 servings.

Grandma & Katie's Frozen Dessert
Jennifer Brown, Garden Grove, CA

1/2 c. creamy peanut
  butter
1/2 c. light corn syrup
2 c. crispy rice cereal
2 c. chocolate-flavored
  crispy rice cereal
1/2 gal. vanilla ice cream,
  softened
1/2 to 1 c. Spanish peanuts
Garnish: chocolate syrup

Blend together peanut butter and corn syrup in a large bowl. Add cereals; stir until coated. Press into the bottom of a ungreased 13"x9" baking pan. Spread ice cream over cereal mixture; sprinkle with peanuts. Swirl chocolate syrup over top. Cover with aluminum foil; freeze at least 4 hours before serving. Cut into squares to serve. Makes 15 to 18 servings.

First-Prize Peach Cobbler

Mom-Mom's Famous Apple Crisp

Mom-Mom's Famous Apple Crisp

Marion Satterthwaite, Blairstown, NJ

10 apples, peeled, cored   1 c. water
  and quartered

Arrange apple slices in an ungreased 8"x8" baking pan, filling pan tightly. Pour water over apples; set aside. Spoon topping over apples. Bake at 325 degrees for 1-1/2 to 2 hours, until apples are very tender and topping is golden. Makes 6 to 8 servings.

Topping:

3/4 c. brown sugar, packed   1/2 c. butter, softened
1 t. cinnamon

Combine ingredients; mix with a pastry blender until crumbly. Topping may be doubled for added sweetness.

Brownies à la Mode

Judy Borecky, Escondido, CA

1-1/2 c. all-purpose flour   1/2 c. chocolate chips
1/2 t. baking powder   1/4 c. chopped nuts
1/2 t. salt   Garnish: vanilla ice cream,
1/3 c. baking cocoa   caramel ice cream
2 c. sugar   topping and chocolate
1 c. butter, softened   syrup
4 eggs, beaten

Combine the first 5 ingredients together; toss gently to mix. Stir in butter and eggs; blend well. Spread batter into a greased 13"x9" baking pan; sprinkle with chocolate chips and nuts. Bake at 350 degrees for 30 to 35 minutes; cool to lukewarm. Cut into squares and top each with a scoop of ice cream; drizzle with caramel topping and chocolate syrup. Makes 2 dozen.

Chocolate Icebox Cake

Joan Trefethen, Fairborn, OH

3.4-oz. pkg. cook & serve   2 sleeves graham crackers,
  vanilla pudding   divided
3.4-oz. pkg. cook & serve   Garnish: whipped cream,
  chocolate pudding   chocolate sprinkles
3 c. milk, divided

Prepare pudding mixes separately as packages direct, using 1-1/2 cups milk for each one. Let puddings cool slightly. Line the bottom of an ungreased 13"x9" baking pan with whole crackers. Line sides of pan with halved crackers. Spoon vanilla pudding over crackers. Cover with another layer of whole crackers; spoon chocolate pudding over crackers. Crumble remaining crackers over top. Refrigerate until chilled. At serving time, dollop individual portions with whipped cream; garnish with sprinkles. Serves 8 to 10.

Quick tip

A quick and yummy dip for fresh fruit: combine a 14-ounce bag of unwrapped caramels with a 5-ounce can of evaporated milk, 1/2 cup chocolate chips and 1/2 teaspoon vanilla extract in a 2-quart casserole dish. Bake at 350 degrees for 30 minutes, until melted and smooth.

Sweet Treat Desserts

Social Apple Betty

Barb Rudyk, Alberta, Canada

6 to 7 apples, peeled, cored, and sliced
cinnamon to taste
Optional: sugar to taste
1/2 c. butter, softened
1 c. brown sugar, packed
3/4 c. all-purpose flour

Arrange sliced apples in an ungreased 1-1/2 quart casserole dish, filling 2/3 full. Sprinkle with cinnamon to taste. If apples are tart, add some sugar, as desired. In a bowl, blend butter and brown sugar. Add flour; mix with a fork until crumbly. Sprinkle butter mixture over apples; pat firmly into a crust. Bake at 325 degrees for 40 minutes, or until golden and apples are tender. Serve warm. Serves 6.

Social Apple Betty

Spiced Cranberry-Apple Crisp

Arlene Smulski, Lyons, IL

4 Golden Delicious apples, peeled, cored and sliced
1 c. fresh cranberries
3/4 c. light brown sugar, packed
1/2 c. all-purpose flour
1/2 c. rolled oats, uncooked
3/4 t. cinnamon
3/4 t. nutmeg
1/3 c. butter, softened
Garnish: ice cream or whipped cream

Combine apples and cranberries in a buttered 8"x8" baking pan; set aside. In a bowl, combine remaining ingredients except garnish. Mix well and sprinkle over fruit. Bake at 375 degrees for 30 minutes, or until top is golden. Serve warm; garnish with ice cream or whipped cream. Makes 6 servings.

Graham Cracker Apple Crisp

Evie Prevo, Livermore, CA

8 Granny Smith apples, peeled, cored and sliced
1/2 c. water
1-1/4 c. sugar, divided
1 c. graham cracker crumbs
1/2 c. all-purpose flour
1 t. cinnamon
1/8 t. salt
1/2 c. butter, melted

Arrange apple slices in a buttered 11"x7" baking pan. Use more or less apples depending on their size; pan should be nearly full to the top but not heaping. Mix water and 1/2 cup sugar together; sprinkle over apples. Mix remaining sugar, graham cracker crumbs, flour, cinnamon and salt and sprinkle over apples. Drizzle melted butter evenly over topping. Bake at 450 degrees for 10 minutes; lower heat to 350 degrees and bake for an additional 40 minutes. Serves 8 to 10.

Spiced Cranberry-Apple Crisp

Quebec Maple Bread Pudding

French Pear Pudding

Kathleen Walker, Mountain Center, CA

8-oz. container sour cream
1 egg, lightly beaten
1 t. vanilla extract
2 T. sugar
1/3 c. plus 1 T. all-purpose
  flour, divided

15-oz. can pear halves,
  drained and quartered
1/4 c. brown sugar, packed
1/2 t. nutmeg
2 T. butter

In a bowl, combine sour cream, egg and vanilla. In a cup, mix sugar and one tablespoon flour; add to sour cream mixture and stir well. Arrange pears in an ungreased shallow one-quart casserole dish; top with sour cream mixture. Bake at 350 degrees for 15 minutes. In a separate bowl, combine brown sugar, remaining flour and nutmeg. Cut in butter with a pastry blender until mixture resembles cornmeal. Sprinkle over sour cream mixture; bake an additional 15 minutes. Makes 6 servings.

French Pear Pudding

Quebec Maple Bread Pudding

Mitzy LaFrenais-Hafner, Quebec, Canada

3 c. egg bread or white
  bread, cubed
Optional: 1/2 c. chopped
  pecans or walnuts
3 c. milk
1 c. brown sugar, packed

4 eggs, beaten
1 t. vanilla extract
2 T. butter, sliced
Garnish: pure maple syrup

Place bread cubes in a greased 2-quart casserole dish. Sprinkle with nuts, if using; set aside. Combine milk and brown sugar in a saucepan over medium-low heat; stir until hot and sugar is dissolved. Remove from heat. Whisk in eggs; stir in vanilla. Pour milk mixture over bread, soaking thoroughly. Dot with butter. Bake at 350 degrees for one hour, or until set. Serve warm, drizzled generously with maple syrup. Serves 4.

Amish Cream Pie

Kristen Cook, Avon Lake, OH

1/3 c. all-purpose flour
1/2 c. butter, melted
1 c. brown sugar, packed
1 pt. whipping cream

9-inch pie crust or graham
  cracker crust
Garnish: whipped cream

In a large bowl, blend flour into melted butter. Add brown sugar; mix thoroughly. Add cream and stir until well blended. Pour into crust. Bake at 375 degrees for 50 to 55 minutes, until center is jiggly but not liquid. Cool. Serve with whipped cream. Serves 6 to 8.

Blueberry Buckle

Blueberry Buckle

Karen Bernards, San Fernando, CA

1-1/4 c. sugar, divided	2 t. baking powder
1/2 c. butter, softened and divided	1/2 t. salt
1 egg, beaten	2 c. fresh blueberries
1/2 c. milk	1/2 t. cinnamon
2-1/3 c. all-purpose flour, divided	

Mix 3/4 cup sugar, 1/4 cup butter and egg; stir in milk. Sift together 2 cups flour, baking powder and salt; add to batter. Blend in blueberries. Spread batter in a greased 2-quart casserole dish. In a separate bowl, mix cinnamon and remaining sugar, flour and butter until crumbly. Sprinkle cinnamon mixture over blueberry mixture. Bake at 375 degrees for 35 to 40 minutes, until bubbly and golden. Serves 9.

Cranberry-Walnut Cobbler

Kathy Grashoff, Fort Wayne, IN

2-1/2 c. fresh or frozen cranberries	3/4 c. butter, melted and slightly cooled
3/4 c. chopped walnuts	1/4 t. almond extract
1/2 c. plus 3/4 c. sugar, divided	1 c. all-purpose flour
2 eggs, beaten	1/8 t. salt

In an ungreased 9" pie plate, combine cranberries, walnuts and 1/2 cup sugar. Toss until coated; set aside. In a bowl, whisk together eggs, melted butter, remaining sugar and extract until blended. Fold in flour and salt until combined. Pour batter over cranberry mixture. Bake at 350 degrees for 40 minutes, or until bubbly and crust is golden. Transfer to a wire rack to cool. Serves 8.

Mom's Blackberry Crisp

Pat Gilmer, West Linn, OR

3/4 c. sugar, divided	1/8 t. salt
3/4 c. plus 1 T. all-purpose flour, divided	1/3 c. margarine
1 t. cinnamon, divided	1/4 c. chopped walnuts
5 to 6 c. blackberries	Optional: 1/4 t. orange or lemon zest

Combine 1/4 cup sugar, 4 to 5 tablespoons flour and 1/2 teaspoon cinnamon; gently fold into berries. Spread in a greased 9" pie plate. Combine remaining sugar, flour and cinnamon; add salt. Cut in margarine a little at a time with a fork or pastry blender. Add chopped nuts and zest, if using. Sprinkle topping over berries. Bake at 400 degrees for about 20 minutes, or until golden. Makes 4 to 6 servings.

Cranberry-Walnut Cobbler

Country Rhubarb Crunch

Harvest Apple Cheesecake

Brenda Smith, Delaware, OH

2 c. graham cracker crumbs

1/3 c. brown sugar, packed

1/2 c. butter, melted and divided

1 T. cinnamon

3 apples, peeled, cored and sliced into 12 rings

4 eggs, beaten

3/4 c. sugar

8-oz. container ricotta cheese

8-oz. pkg. cream cheese, softened

2 t. vanilla extract

8-oz. container whipping cream

Garnish: cinnamon

Combine cracker crumbs, brown sugar, 1/4 cup butter and cinnamon. Press onto bottom and partway up sides of an ungreased 9" springform pan. In a skillet, sauté apple slices on both sides in remaining butter. Arrange 6 apple slices on prepared crust. In a bowl, beat eggs, sugar, ricotta cheese, cream cheese and vanilla until smooth. Add whipping cream and blend well. Pour cheese mixture into pan. Arrange remaining apple slices on top and press apples slightly under the mixture. Sprinkle top with cinnamon. Bake at 450 degrees for 10 minutes, then reduce heat to 300 degrees and bake for 50 to 55 minutes. Cool and refrigerate overnight. Serves 8 to 12.

Quick tip

To keep a chilled dessert cool on a warm day, just fill a picnic basket with plastic zipping bags full of ice, lay a colorful tablecloth over the ice and set the sweets on top.

Country Rhubarb Crunch

Terri Clark, Huber Heights, OH

1 c. plus 2 T. all-purpose flour, divided

2 c. sugar, divided

1 T. butter, diced

4 c. rhubarb, sliced

1 t. baking powder

1/4 t. salt

1 egg, beaten

Garnish: vanilla ice cream

In a large bowl, mix together 2 tablespoons flour, one cup sugar, butter and rhubarb. Spoon into an ungreased 1-1/2 quart casserole dish. In a separate bowl, mix together remaining flour, remaining sugar, baking powder and salt. Stir in egg. Mixture will be crumbly. Sprinkle over rhubarb mixture; shake pan so crumbs settle into rhubarb. Bake at 350 degrees for 40 minutes, or until crust is lightly golden. Serve warm or cold, topped with scoops of vanilla ice cream. Makes 8 servings.

Harvest Apple Cheesecake

Sweet Treat Desserts

Wash-Day Peach Pie
Jennifer Bryant, Bowling Green, KY

1 c. self-rising flour
1 c. sugar
1 c. milk
15-oz. can sliced peaches, drained
1/4 c. butter, sliced
Garnish: vanilla ice cream or whipped topping

Stir together flour and sugar; add milk and stir until smooth. Pour batter into a greased 1-1/2 quart casserole dish; spoon peaches over top. Place butter in center. Bake at 350 degrees for one hour, or until golden. Serve warm, topped with ice cream or whipped topping. Makes 8 servings.

Pineapple Upside-Down Cake
Cathy Clemons, Narrows, VA

6 T. butter
1 c. brown sugar, packed
20-oz. can pineapple slices, drained
8 to 10 maraschino cherries
18-1/2 oz. pkg. yellow cake mix
3 eggs, beaten
1/3 c. oil
20-oz. can crushed pineapple
Garnish: whipped cream

Melt butter in a 13"x9" baking pan in a 350-degree oven. Remove pan from oven; sprinkle brown sugar over butter. Arrange pineapple slices decoratively in pan; fill in spaces with cherries and set aside. In a large bowl, combine dry cake mix, eggs, oil and crushed pineapple with its juice. Beat with an electric mixer on high speed for 2 minutes. Pour batter over pineapple slices. Bake at 350 degrees for 40 minutes, or until cake tests done. Remove from oven; allow to cool 10 to 15 minutes in pan. Place a serving platter onto pan and very carefully invert cake onto platter. Serve warm or at room temperature, topped with whipped cream. Makes 16 servings.

Strawberry-Nectarine Cobbler
Alisha Jhai, West Dundee, IL

6 to 8 nectarines, pitted and very thinly sliced
1/4 c. light brown sugar, packed
1 t. cinnamon
1/4 t. nutmeg
1 t. salt
2 c. fresh strawberries, hulled and halved or whole
2 T. butter, sliced
1/2 c. sugar, divided
1 egg, beaten
1 T. baking powder
1 c. all-purpose flour
1 T. vanilla extract
1/2 c. milk

Combine nectarines, brown sugar, spices and salt; let stand for 15 minutes. In a saucepan, combine strawberries, butter and 1/4 cup sugar. Cook and stir for 5 minutes, until syrupy. Remove from heat; cool. In a separate bowl, whisk remaining sugar, egg, baking powder, flour, vanilla and milk. Spread nectarine mixture evenly in an ungreased 13"x9" glass baking pan. Spoon strawberry mixture evenly over nectarines. Dollop with spoonfuls of batter. Bake at 350 degrees for 30 to 35 minutes. Cool at least 15 minutes. Serves 12.

Quick tip
Generally, you can reuse parchment paper at least once. When it starts to darken and dry out, toss it.

Strawberry-Nectarine Cobbler

Shiny-Top Blueberry Cobbler

Shiny-Top Blueberry Cobbler

Bonnie Russell, Dixon, CA

5 to 6 c. fresh blueberries
1-1/2 T. lemon juice
2 c. all-purpose flour
2 c. sugar, divided
2 t. baking powder
1 t. salt, divided
1 c. milk
1/3 c. butter, diced
2 T. cornstarch
1-1/2 c. boiling water
Garnish: vanilla ice cream

Spread berries in a greased shallow 2-1/2 quart casserole dish. Sprinkle with lemon juice; set aside. In a bowl, combine flour, one cup sugar, baking powder, 1/2 teaspoon salt, milk and butter. Stir until well blended. Spoon batter over berries, spreading to edge of dish; set aside. In a small bowl, mix remaining sugar and salt with cornstarch. Sprinkle over batter. Pour boiling water over all; do not stir. Bake at 350 degrees for one hour, or until bubbly, golden and glazed. Serve warm or cooled, topped with ice cream. Serves 10 to 12.

Sour Cream Kuchen

Catherine Blatnik, Okemos, MI

1 c. butter, softened
1 c. sugar
2 eggs, beaten
1 t. vanilla extract
2 c. all-purpose flour
1 t. baking powder
1 t. baking soda
1/2 t. salt
8-oz. container sour cream

In a large bowl, beat butter and sugar with an electric mixer on medium speed until smooth. Add remaining ingredients; mix well. Spread half of batter in an ungreased 13"x9" baking pan. Cover with half of topping. Repeat with remaining batter and topping. Bake at 350 degrees for 35 to 40 minutes, until a toothpick tests clean. Cool about 15 minutes. Serves 10 to 12.

Topping:

1/2 c. brown sugar, packed
1/3 c. sugar
2 t. cinnamon

Mix all ingredients well.

Sour Cream Kuchen

Quick tip

If you're out of half-and-half, substitute 4-1/2 teaspoons melted butter plus enough milk to equal one cup. You can also use an equal amount of evaporated milk.

Pumpkin Custard Crunch

Donna Borton, Columbus, OH

29-oz. can pumpkin
3 eggs, beaten
2 t. pumpkin pie spice
1 t. cinnamon

14-oz. can sweetened
  condensed milk
1 c. milk
2 t. vanilla extract

Mix pumpkin, eggs and spices well; stir in milks and vanilla. Pour into a greased 13"x9" baking pan; spoon crunch topping over pumpkin mixture. Bake at 350 degrees for 45 to 60 minutes, until a knife tip comes out clean. Watch carefully so that topping doesn't burn. Serve warm. Makes 9 to 12 servings.

Crunch Topping:

3 c. quick-cooking oats,
  uncooked
1 c. brown sugar, packed
1 c. all-purpose flour

1 t. cinnamon
1 c. walnuts or pecans,
  crushed
1 c. butter, melted

Stir together oats, brown sugar, flour, cinnamon and nuts. Add melted butter; toss to mix.

Pumpkin Custard Crunch

Creamy Coconut Bread Pudding

Patty Parker, Cabool, MO

8-oz. pkg. cream cheese,
  room temperature
1 c. sugar
4 eggs, beaten
2 c. milk
15-oz. can cream of
  coconut
5 T. butter, melted and
  divided

1/2 loaf French bread,
  cubed
1/2 c. sweetened flaked
  coconut
1/2 c. chopped pecans
Garnish: whipped cream

In a large bowl, beat cream cheese until creamy. Add sugar and eggs; beat again. Stir in milk, cream of coconut and 2 tablespoons melted butter. Stir in bread cubes; let stand a few minutes, until moistened. Spoon mixture into a buttered 13"x9" baking pan. Bake at 350 degrees for 35 minutes; do not overbake. Combine coconut, pecans and remaining butter; sprinkle over top. Bake another 5 to 8 minutes, until golden. For best flavor, chill before serving. Garnish with whipped cream. Serves 12 to 15.

Coconut Fridge Cake

Jennifer Holcomb, Port Angeles, WA

18-1/2 oz. pkg. white cake
  mix
16-oz. container frozen
  whipped topping, thawed
8-oz. container sour cream

1 c. sweetened flaked
  coconut
1 c. sugar

Prepare cake mix according to package directions, baking in two, 9" round baking pans. Cool; slice each layer horizontally in half to make 4 layers. To make frosting, mix remaining ingredients together well. Frost and stack layers on a cake plate; frost top and sides of cake with remaining frosting. Cover and refrigerate cake for one to 3 days before serving, as flavor improves with age. Serves 8 to 10.

Creamy Coconut Bread Pudding

Cherry Crumb Dessert

Cherry Crumb Dessert

Charlotte Smith, Alexandria, PA

1/2 c. butter, chilled
18-1/2 oz. pkg. yellow cake mix
21-oz. can cherry pie filling
1/2 c. chopped walnuts
Garnish: vanilla ice cream

In a large bowl, cut butter into dry cake mix until mixture resembles coarse crumbs. Set aside one cup of mixture for topping. Pat remaining mixture into the bottom of a greased 13"x9" baking pan and 1/2 inch up the sides to form a crust. Spread pie filling over crust. Combine nuts with remaining crumbs; sprinkle over top. Bake at 350 degrees for 30 to 35 minutes. Serve warm, topped with ice cream. Makes 12 servings.

Cherry Brownie Cobbler

Amy Hunt, Traphill, NC

20-oz. pkg. brownie mix
1/2 c. water
1/2 c. oil
1 egg, beaten
21-oz. can cherry pie filling
1/4 c. butter, softened
8-1/2 oz. pkg. yellow cake mix
Garnish: vanilla ice cream

Prepare brownie mix according to packaging directions, using water, oil and egg. Spread batter into a 13"x9" baking pan sprayed with non-stick vegetable spray. Bake at 350 degrees for 15 minutes; remove from oven. Spread pie filling over brownie layer; set aside. Cut butter into dry cake mix until crumbly. Sprinkle mixture over pie filling. Return to oven and continue to bake an additional 45 to 50 minutes, until filling is set. Cool completely; cut into squares. Serve topped with scoops of ice cream. Serves 10 to 12.

Mocha Pudding Cake

Lanita Anderson, Chesapeake, VA

1 c. all-purpose flour
1 c. sugar, divided
6 T. baking cocoa, divided
1-1/2 t. baking powder
1/4 t. salt
1/2 c. milk
3 T. oil
1 t. vanilla extract
1/2 c. mini semi-sweet chocolate chips
1 c. brewed strong coffee
Garnish: vanilla ice cream or whipped topping

Combine flour, 2/3 cup sugar, 4 tablespoons cocoa, baking powder and salt in a large bowl. In a separate bowl, stir together milk, oil and vanilla. Add to dry ingredients, stirring just until blended. Spread batter evenly into a lightly greased 8"x8" baking pan. Combine chocolate chips with remaining sugar and cocoa; sprinkle evenly over batter. Bring coffee to a boil; pour evenly over batter. Do not stir. Bake at 350 degrees for 25 to 30 minutes, or until cake springs back when lightly pressed in center. Garnish as desired. Serves 8 to 10.

Quick tip

One fewer dish to clean...melt the butter right in the baking pan as the oven preheats! Just remember to keep an eye on it so the butter doesn't scorch.

Honey-Custard Bread Pudding

Rogene Rogers, Bemidji, MN

6 eggs

1/2 t. salt

4 c. milk

2/3 c. plus 2 T. honey, divided

2 T. butter, melted

Optional: 1/2 c. raisins

16-oz. loaf Vienna or French bread, torn into one-inch pieces

Beat together eggs and salt; set aside. Bring milk just to a boil in a saucepan over low heat; let cool slightly. Stir 2/3 cup honey and butter into milk. Slowly stir eggs into milk mixture; add raisins, if using. Place bread pieces in a greased 2-1/2 quart casserole dish. Pour egg mixture over bread. Set casserole dish in a larger pan; add hot water to the pan to come halfway up the side of the casserole dish. Bake at 325 degrees for one hour, or until set. About 15 minutes before serving, drizzle remaining honey over top. Makes 8 to 10 servings.

Honey-Custard Bread Pudding

Prize Peanut Butter-Chocolate Dessert

Deborah Price, La Rue, OH

20 chocolate sandwich cookies, divided

2 T. butter, melted

8-oz. pkg. cream cheese, softened

1/2 c. creamy peanut butter

1-1/2 c. powdered sugar, divided

16-oz. container frozen whipped topping, thawed and divided

15 mini peanut butter cups, chopped

1 c. cold milk

3.9-oz. pkg. instant chocolate fudge pudding mix

Crush 16 cookies; toss with butter. Press into the bottom of an ungreased 9"x9" baking pan. In a bowl, beat cream cheese, peanut butter and one cup powdered sugar until smooth. Fold in half of the whipped topping; spread over crust. Sprinkle with peanut butter cups. In a separate bowl, beat milk, dry pudding mix and remaining powdered sugar on low speed for 2 minutes. Fold in remaining topping; spread over peanut butter cups. Crush remaining cookies; sprinkle over top. Cover and chill at least 3 hours. Serves 12 to 15.

Quick tip

To easily clean strawberries, place them in a sink filled with water and gently wash with the sprayer nozzle on the sink. The water from the nozzle will toss and turn the strawberries, giving them a thorough cleaning.

Prize Peanut Butter-Chocolate Dessert

Sweet Treat Desserts

Oh-So-Easy Peach Cobbler

Dueley Lucas, Somerset, KY

2 15-oz. cans sliced
   peaches, drained and
   1/2 c. juice reserved
1/2 c. butter, sliced

1 c. self-rising flour
1 c. sugar
1 c. milk

Arrange peaches in a 13"x9" baking pan that has been
sprayed with non-stick vegetable spray. Pour in reserved
juice. Place butter slices over peaches. In a bowl, mix
flour, sugar and milk, stirring until smooth. Pour over
peaches, spreading batter to the edges of pan. Bake
at 375 degrees for 30 minutes, or until golden.
Serves 10 to 12.

Quick tip

Company on the way? A frozen pound cake
topped with a can of favorite-flavor fruit pie
filling and frozen whipped topping makes
a simple and delicious dessert in minutes!
Serve slices on your prettiest china.

Oh-So-Easy Peach Cobbler

Royal Strawberry Shortcake

Becky Smith, North Canton, OH

1/4 c. butter, softened
3/4 c. sugar
1 egg, beaten
2 c. all-purpose flour
4 t. baking powder
1/8 t. salt
1 c. milk
2 t. vanilla extract
3 to 4 c. fresh strawberries, hulled and sliced
Optional: softened cream cheese
Garnish: whipped cream

In a large bowl, blend together butter and sugar. Add egg; mix well. In a separate bowl, combine flour, baking powder and salt. Add flour mixture to butter mixture alternately with milk. Stir in vanilla. Spread batter in a greased 13"x9" baking pan. Bake at 350 degrees for 25 to 30 minutes. Cool; cut shortcake into squares and split. Place bottom halves of shortcake squares on dessert plates. Spread with cream cheese, if desired; top with strawberries and whipped cream. Add shortcake tops and more berries and cream. Serves 10 to 12.

Martha's Shredded Apple Pie

Patti Walker, Mocksville, NC

8 Granny Smith apples, peeled, cored and shredded
1/4 t. lemon juice
1-1/2 t. apple pie spice
2 9-inch pie crusts
1/2 c. butter, melted
2 c. sugar
3 eggs, beaten
nutmeg to taste

Place apples in a large bowl; toss with lemon juice and spice. Pierce unbaked crusts lightly with a fork; fill with apples. Mix melted butter, sugar and eggs; pour mixture evenly over apples. Dust the top of each pie with a dash of nutmeg. Bake at 350 degrees for 45 minutes to an hour. Allow to cool (if you can wait!) before slicing. Makes 2 pies, 8 servings each.

Royal Strawberry Shortcake

Sweet Cinnamon Pie

Janet McRoberts, Lexington, KY

1/2 T. all-purpose flour
3 T. sugar
2 T. cinnamon
2 T. butter, softened
3 eggs, beaten
2 c. milk
9-inch pie crust

Mix flour, sugar, cinnamon and butter together. Stir in eggs and milk; pour into unbaked pie crust. Bake at 350 degrees for 45 to 50 minutes, until set. Cool before slicing. Serves 8.

INDEX

INDEX

INDEX

INDEX

Send us your favorite recipe

...and the memory that makes it special for you!*
If we select your recipe for a brand-new **Gooseberry Patch** cookbook, your name will appear right along with it...and you'll receive a FREE copy of the book!

Submit your recipe on our website at www.gooseberrypatch.com/sharearecipe or mail to: Gooseberry Patch, PO Box 812, Columbus, OH 43216

*Please include the number of servings and all other necessary information.

Have a taste for more?

Visit www.gooseberrypatch.com to join our Circle of Friends!
- Free recipes, tips and ideas plus a complete cookbook index
- Get special email offers and our monthly eLetter delivered to your inbox